TEST YOUR JAVA SKILLS

Mahavir DS Rathore

Books by Mahavir DS Rathore

   a. Java 8 Exception Handling
   b. Java 8 Exception Handling Quiz
   c. Learn Java 8 in a Week

Copyright

About the author

I have has been programming and teaching Java for last 18 years. This book is an effort to share my experience with everyone across the world. I am available for public speaking, workshops and training on Java anywhere in the world.
My email id is gurumahaveer@gmail.com .

Who should read the book?

This book is for programmers who already know Core Java programming language and are keen to deepen their knowledge further.

Acknowledgement

Java is owned by Oracle and trademark is acknowledged.

Dedication

To my Kakosa Shri. Samdar Singh Rathore.

Feedback

Please share your feedback which will help me to improve this book.

Table of Content

Chapter 1
What is Java?

Q.1: What is the latest version of Java?	
A	7
B	6
C	9
D	8
	<----Right Answer

Q.2: Identify the incorrect statement.	
A	Java is programming language.
B	Java is a platform.
C	Java is dynamically typed.
D	Java is statically typed.
	<----Right Answer

Q.3: JDK stands for	
A	Java Development Kit.
B	Java Developer Kit.
C	Java Database Kit.
D	Java Data Kit.
	<----Right Answer

Q.4: JRE stands for	
A	Java Runtime Execution.
B	Java Runtime Engine.
C	Java Reusable Execution.
D	Java Reusable Engine.
	<----Right Answer

Q.5: Java is a ....

A	Platform.
B	Language.
C	Operating System.
D	Database.
	<----Right Answer

Q.6: 'Tiger' was the code name for which version of Java?

A	5
B	6
C	7
D	8
	<----Right Answer

Q.7: .... Language is not supported by Java platform.

A	Groovy.
B	Java.
C	C++.
D	Scala.
	<----Right Answer

Q.8: .... Language is supported by Java platform

A	Delphi.
B	Kotlin.
C	Swift.
D	VB.Net.
	<----Right Answer

Q.9: .... Is used for development of Web based applications.

A	Java Card.
B	Java Standard Edition.
C	Java Micro Edition.
D	Java Enterprise Edition.
	<----Right Answer

Q.10: JVM stands for	
A	Java Vacuum Machine.
B	Java Void Machine.
C	Java Virtual Machine.
D	Java Virtual Model.
	<----Right Answer

Q.11: Which of the following language(s) is/are not supported on Java platform?	
A	C#.
B	Jython.
C	Kotlin.
D	Java.
	<----Right Answer

Q.12: ....is used for development of set top box and printer applications.	
A	Java Micro Edition.
B	Java Enterprise Edition.
C	Java Standard Edition.
D	Java Card.
	<----Right Answer

Q.13: .... Language is supported by Java platform.	
A	R.
B	Jruby.
C	C.
D	JScala.
	<----Right Answer

Q.14: Identify the correct statement.	
A	Bytecode is processor independent.
B	Bytecode is processor dependent.
C	Bytecode is OS independent.
D	Bytecode is OS dependent.

	<----Right Answer

Q.15: ....Language is supported by Java platform.

A	Scala.
B	C++.
C	Objective C.
D	Javascript.
	<----Right Answer

Q.16: .... Is used for development of desktop applications.

A	Java Enterprise Edition.
B	Java Standard Edition.
C	Java Card.
D	Java Micro Edition.
	<----Right Answer

Q.17: Java is a .... Paradigm programming language.

A	Single.
B	Object.
C	Multi.
D	Functional.
	<----Right Answer

Q.18: Java has been influenced by ....

A	VB.Net.
B	Objective C.
C	C++.
D	R.
	<----Right Answer

Q.19: .... Language is supported by Java platform.

A	D.
B	Cobol.
C	Pascal.

D	Groovy.
	<----Right Answer

Q.20: Java language supports .... typing.

A	Dynamic.
B	Static.
C	Hybrid.
D	Meta.
	<----Right Answer

Q.21: Java is owned by ....

A	Microsoft.
B	Google.
C	Oracle.
D	Infosys.
	<----Right Answer

Q.22: ....Is used for smart card applications.

A	Java Card.
B	Java Standard Edition.
C	Java Enterprise Edition.
D	Java Micro Edition.
	<----Right Answer

Q.23: .... Language is influenced by Java.

A	Swift.
B	Hack.
C	Clojure.
D	Make.
	<----Right Answer

Q.24: .... Language is supported by Java platform.

A	JPerl.
B	JPHP.
C	Jython.

D	MongoDB.
	<----Right Answer

Q.25: Identify the correct statement.	
A	Java supports object oriented programming.
B	Java supports concurrent programming.
C	Java supports reflection.
D	None of the above.
	<----Right Answer

Q.26: ....Is the minimum environment required for running a Java program.	
A	JDK.
B	JEE.
C	JRE.
D	JSE.
	<----Right Answer

Q.27: What are the components of JDK?	
A	Compiler.
B	Interpreter.
C	Libraries.
D	Tools.
	<----Right Answer

Q.28: Java has been influenced by	
A	Javascript.
B	Jscript.
C	C#.
D	Hadoop.
	<----Right Answer

Q.29: .... Language has been influenced by Java.	
A	Python.
B	C++.

C	Ada.
D	D.
	<----Right Answer

Q.30: .... Is the minimum environment required for development of Java program.

A	JDK.
B	JRE.
C	Java Kick.
D	Java Development.
	<----Right Answer

Q.31: What are the components of JRE?

A	Interpreter.
B	Libraries (API).
C	Tools.
D	Compiler.
	<----Right Answer

Q.32: On Windows OS in which directory is 32 bit JDK 1.8 is installed by default?

A	C:\Windows\Java.
B	C:\Program Files (x86)\Java\Jdk1.8.xxx.
C	C:\Program Files\Java\Jdk1.8.xxx.
D	C:\Windows\System32.
	<----Right Answer

Q.33: Which of the following is not an IDE?

A	Eclipse.
B	Netbeans.
C	JDeveloper.
D	Notepad++.
	<----Right Answer

Q.34: Java was invented by ....

A	Larry wall.
B	James Gosling.
C	Anders Hejlsberg.
D	Nandan Nilkeni.
	<----Right Answer

Q.35: Java is a .... Language.

A	Functional.
B	Object Oriented.
C	Markup.
D	Structured.
	<----Right Answer

Q.36: .... Is used for development of distributed applications.

A	Java Standard Edition.
B	Java Micro Edition.
C	Java Enterprise Edition.
D	Java Card.
	<----Right Answer

Q.37: When was version 1.0 of Java released?

A	1995
B	1994
C	1996
D	1993
	<----Right Answer

Q.38: Which of the following is not a code editor?

A	Notepad++.
B	jEdit.
C	Notepad.
D	Netbeans.
	<----Right Answer

Q.39: On Windows OS in which directory is 64 bit JDK1.8 is installed

by default?	
A	C:\Windows.
B	C:\Program Files (x86)\Java\Jdk1.8.xxx.
C	C:\Windows\System64.
D	C:\Program Files\Java\Jdk1.8.xxx.
	<----Right Answer

Q.40: What was the codename for Java 1.0?	
A	Oak.
B	Merlin.
C	Mustang.
D	Delta.
	<----Right Answer

Answers:

Q.No	Ans	Explanation
1	D	The latest version of Java is 8.
2	C	Java is statically typed.
3	A	JDK stands for Java Development Kit.
4	B	JRE stands for Java Runtime Engine.
5	A,B	Java is both a Platform and Langauge.
6	A	Tiger was code name for Java 5.
7	C	C++ is not supported on Java Platform.
8	B	Kotlin language is supported on Java platform.
9	D	JEE is used for development of web based apps using Java.
10	C	JVM Stands for Java Virtual Machine.
11	A	C# is not supported by Java platform.
12	A	Java ME is used for development of setup box and printer apps.
13	B	JRuby is supported on Java platform.
14	A,C	Bytecode is OS and Processor independent.
15	A	Scala is supported by Java platform.

16	C	Java SE is used for developing desktop applications.
17	C	Java is a multi-paradigm language.
18	C	Java has been influenced by C++.
19	D	Groovy is supported by Java platform.
20	B	Java is statically typed.
21	C	Java is owned by oracle.
22	A	Java card is used for development of smart card apps.
23	C	Clojure is influenced by Java.
24	C	Jython is supported on Java platform.
25	A,B, C	Java has support for OOP, concurrent programming and reflection.
26	C	JRE is the minimum environment required for running Java apps.
27	A,B, C,D	JDK is composed of Compiler, Interpreter, Tools and Library (API).
28	C	Java has been influenced by C# from version 5 onwards.
29	A	Python has been influenced by Java.
30	A	JDK is required for developing Java apps at the minimum.
31	A,B, C	JRE is composed of Interpreter, Tools, Library(API).
32	B	32-bit JDK1.8 is installed in C:\Program Files (x86)\Java\Jdk1.8.xxx directory on Windows OS by default.
33	D	Notepad++ is a code editor.
34	B	James gosling invented Java.
35	B	Java is object oriented programming language.
36	C	Java EE is used for development of distributed Java apps.
37	C	Java 1.0 was released in year 1996.
38	D	NetBeans is an IDE.
39	D	64-bit JDK1.8 is installed in C:\Program Files\Java\Jdk1.8.xxx directory by default on a Windows OS.
40	A	"Oak" was the codename for Java 1.0 .

Chapter 2
Java Compiler and Java Interpreter

Q.1: Which of the following is the Java compiler?	
A	Java.exe.
B	Javac.exe.
C	Javap.exe.
D	Javaci.exe.
	<----Right Answer

Q.2: Which of the following is the Java interpreter?	
A	Javai.exe.
B	Javat.exe.
C	Javac.exe.
D	Java.exe.
	<----Right Answer

Q.3: .... Environment variable identifies the location of Java compiler?	
A	CLASSPATH.
B	PATH.
C	JAVAPATH.
D	COMPILERPATH.
	<----Right Answer

Q.4: How to get detailed compilation information when compiling a Java program?	
A	Javac –info.
B	Javac –verbose.
C	Javac –information.

D	Javac –data.
	<----Right Answer

Q.5: How to get version of the Java interpreter?

A	Java –v.
B	Java –version.
C	Java –ver.
D	Java –info.
	<----Right Answer

Q.6: PATH environment variable can be set using?

A	Command line.
B	Control Panel.
C	Editor.
D	Java compiler.
	<----Right Answer

Q.7: How to display value of PATH environment variable at command line?

A	PATH.
B	Set PATH.
C	Show PATH.
D	Display PATH.
	<----Right Answer

Q.8: PATH environment variable can be set to a permanent state using ....

A	Command Line.
B	Control Panel.
C	Java compiler.
D	Java Interpreter.
	<----Right Answer

Q.9: Java compiler options are case sensitive?

A	TRUE.

B	FALSE.
	<----Right Answer

Q.10: How to get all compiler options for the Java compiler?	
A	Javac –help.
B	Javac –h.
C	Javac -?.
D	Javac /?.
	<----Right Answer

Q.11: Identify the correct command	
A	Set path= "C:\Program Files\Java\jdk1.8.0_65\bin".
B	Set PATH = "C:\Program Files\Java\jdk1.8.0_65\bin".
C	Set PATH = %path%; "C:\Program Files\Java\jdk1.8.0_65\bin".
D	All of the above.
	<----Right Answer

Q.12: When a Java program is compiled it generates	
A	Native code.
B	Bytecode.
C	IL.
D	Source code.
	<----Right Answer

Q.13: .... Is used for executing Java bytecode.	
A	Java.exe.
B	Javac.exe.
C	Javai.exe.
D	Javam.exe.
	<----Right Answer

Q.14: Which command is used for setting PATH at command line?	
A	GIVE.
B	SET.
C	ASSIGN.

D	PATH.
	<----Right Answer

Q.15: How to get information on deprecated APIs while compiling?

A	Javac –d.
B	Javac –deprecated.
C	Javac –deprecation.
D	Javac –deprecate.
	<----Right Answer

Q.16: JVM is part of Java compiler.

A	TRUE.
B	FALSE.
	<----Right Answer

Q.17: How to find the version of Java compiler?

A	Javac –version.
B	Javac –Version.
C	Javac –ver.
D	Javac –v.
	<----Right Answer

Q.18: PATH environment variable identifies the location of ....

A	Java compiler.
B	Java interpreter.
C	Java tools.
D	All of the above.
	<----Right Answer

Q.19: Java interpreter options are case sensitive.

A	TRUE.
B	FALSE.
	<----Right Answer

Q.20: JVM is also called as	
A	Java Interpreter.
B	Java Compiler.
C	JIT.
D	All of the above.
	<----Right Answer

Q.21: .... Environment variable identifies the location of Java interpreter.	
A	CLASSPATH.
B	PATH.
C	DATAPATH.
D	JAVAPATH.
	<----Right Answer

Answers:

Q.No	Ans	Explanation
1	B	"Javac.exe" is the Java compiler.
2	D	"Java.exe" is the Java interpreter.
3	B	PATH environment identifies the location of Java compiler.
4	B	"Javac.exe –verbose" command will provide detailed compilation information when compiling.
5	B	"Java –version" will return the version of the interpreter.
6	A,B	PATH environment variable can be set using command line or control panel.
7	B	"SET PATH" command is used for displaying value of PATH environment variable.
8	B	Control panel is used for setting the value of PATH environment permanently.
9	A	Java compiler options are case sensitive.
10	A	Javac –help displays all the compiler options of the Java compiler options.
11	D	All options are correct and valid commands.

12	B	Java compiler compiles source code to byte code.
13	A	Java interpreter is used for executing the bytecode.
14	B	"SET" command is used for setting PATH at command line.
15	C	"Javac –deprecation" returns list of deprecated API (Functions that are will not be supported in future versions of Java).
16	B	Java compiler does not have JVM as a component.
17	A	"Javac –version" will return the version of the java compiler.
18	D	All options are correct.
19	A	Java interpreter options are case sensitive.
20	A	JVM is also called as Java interpreter.
21	B	PATH environment variable identifies the location of Java interpreter.

Chapter 3
HelloWorld Program - I

Q.1: What is the valid extension of a Java program?	
A	.Java
B	.JAVA
C	.JJ
D	None of the above.
	<----Right Answer

Q.2: Identify the correct statement.	
A	Java program file extension is case sensitive.
B	Java program file extension is case sensitive only on Mac OS.
C	Java program file extension is not case sensitive.
D	None of the above.
	<----Right Answer

Q.3: What will happen if a Java program by name of "Prg.ca" is compiled?	
A	Compiler error.
B	No compiler error.
C	Runtime error.
D	None of the above.
	<----Right Answer

Q.4: How to give single line comment?	
A	//
B	#
C	\"
D	/
	<----Right Answer

Q.5: How to give multi-line comment?	
A	//
B	#
C	/* .. */
D	\"\"
	<----Right Answer

Q.6: What will happen if a Java program by name of "Prg.jAva" is compiled?	
A	Runtime error.
B	Compiler error.
C	Data error.
D	None of the above.
	<----Right Answer

Q.7: MyPrg.java will compile to .... file.	
A	MyPrg.class
B	MyPrg.bytecode
C	MyPrg
D	MyPrg.java
	<----Right Answer

Q.8: Binary Java code is also called as	
A	Source code.
B	Byte code.
C	Runtime code.
D	Native code.
	<----Right Answer

Q.9: What is the valid extension of a Java program?	
A	.Java
B	.java
C	.Java
D	None of the above.

	<----Right Answer

Q.10: What will happen if a Java program by name of "Prg.java" is compiled?

A	Compiler error.
B	Runtime error.
C	No Compiler error.
D	Data error.
	<----Right Answer

Q.11: .... Method is the entry point in a Java program.

A	MAIN().
B	Main().
C	main().
D	None of the above.
	<----Right Answer

Q.12: What is the output?

```
class Program {
 public static void main(String a) {
   System.out.println("HelloWorld");
  }
}
```

A	Runtime error.
B	Compiler error.
C	HelloWorld.
D	No output.
	<----Right Answer

Q.13: Which of the following is the valid entry point in a Java program?

A	public static void main(String ...a).
B	public static void Main(String ...a).
C	public static void main().
D	public static void Main().
	<----Right Answer

Q.14: What is the output?

```
class Program {
 public static void main(String[] a) {
   System.out.println("HelloWorld");
  }
}
```

A	Runtime error.
B	HelloWorld.
C	Compiler error.
D	No output.
	<----Right Answer

Q.15: What is the output if the command line arguments are: Ram Hari ?

```
class Program {
 public static void main(String args[]) {
   System.out.println("HelloWorld " + args[0] +"," + args[1]);
 }
}
```

A	HelloWorld.
B	HelloWorld Ram,Hari.
C	Runtime error.
D	None of the above.
	<----Right Answer

Q.16: What is the output (When no command line arguments are passed)?

```
class Program {
 public static void main(String args[]){
  System.out.println("Namaskar :"+ args);
  }
}
```

A	Compiler error.
B	Runtime error.
C	Namaskar :
D	Namaskar :[Ljava.lang.String;@2a139a55
	<----Right Answer

Q.17: What is the output?

```
class Program {
```

```
public static void main(String ...a) {
    System.out.println("HelloWorld");
  }
}
```

A	Compiler error.
B	Runtime error.
C	No output.
D	HelloWorld.
	<----Right Answer

Q.18: Identify the correct signature of "main" method which acts as an entry point?

A	public static void main(String args[]).
B	public static void Main(String args[]).
C	public static void main().
D	public static void Main().
	<----Right Answer

Q.19: What is the output if the command line argument is: Ram?

```
class Program {
 public static void main(String args[]) {
    System.out.println("HelloWorld " + args[0] +"," + args[1]);
  }
}
```

A	HelloWorld Ram.
B	HelloWorld.
C	Compiler error.
D	Runtime error.
	<----Right Answer

Q.20: System class belongs to .... Package.

A	java.lang
B	java.io
C	java.basic
D	java.System
	<----Right Answer

Q.21: What is the output?

```
class Program {
 public static void Main(String args[]) {
   System.out.println("HelloWorld");
  }
}
```

A	Compiler Error.
B	Runtime Error.
C	HelloWorld.
D	No Error.
	<----Right Answer

Q.22: Which of the following is the valid entry point in a Java program?

A	public static void Main(String args[]).
B	public static void main(String[] args).
C	public static void main(String args[]).
D	public static void Main(String[] args).
	<----Right Answer

Q.23: What is the output?

```
class Program {
 public static void main(String args[]) {
   System.out.println("HelloWorld");
  }
}
```

A	Compiler Error.
B	Runtime Error.
C	HelloWorld.
D	No output.
	<----Right Answer

Q.24: What is the Output?

```
class Program {
 public static void main(String args[]) {
   System.out.println("HelloWorld");
  }
 public static void Main(String args[]) {
   System.out.println("HelloWorld");
  }
}
```

A	No output.

B	HelloWorld.
C	Compiler Error.
D	Runtime Error.
	<----Right Answer

Q.25: What is the output?

```
class Program {
 public void static main(String args[]){    System.out.println("Helloworld");
 }
}
```

A	Compiler error.
B	Runtime error.
C	Helloworld.
D	No output.
	<----Right Answer

Q.26: What is the Output?

```
class Program {
 public static void main(String args[]) {
   System.out.println("HelloWorld");
  }
 public static void main(String args[]) {
   System.out.println("HelloWorld");
  }
}
```

A	Runtime error.
B	Compiler error.
C	No output.
D	HelloWorld.
	<----Right Answer

Q.27: "System.out" is an object of .... class.

A	Print.
B	PrintStream.
C	PrintWriter.
D	Printer.
	<----Right Answer

Q.28: What is the output if the command line arguments are: 10 20?

```
class Program {
```

```
public static void main(String args[]) {
        int i = Integer.parseInt(args[0]);
        int j = Integer.parseInt(args[1]);
        System.out.println(i+j);
    }
}
```

A	30
B	Compiler error.
C	Runtime error.
D	10.
	<----Right Answer

Q.29: What is the output?

```
class Program {
 void public static main(String args[]){
  System.out.println("Helloworld");
 }
}
```

A	Compiler error.
B	Runtime error.
C	Helloworld.
D	No output.
	<----Right Answer

Q.30: What is the output if the command line arguments are: A B?

```
class Program {
 public static void main(String args[]) {
        int i = Integer.parseInt(args[0]);
        int j = Integer.parseInt(args[1]);
        System.out.println("The sum is :" + (i+j));
    }
}
```

A	Runtime error.
B	Compiler error.
C	131
D	132
	<----Right Answer

Q.31: What is the output?

```
class Program {
 protected static void main(String args[]){
  System.out.println("Namaskar");
```

}	
}	
A	Namaskar.
B	Compiler error.
C	Runtime error.
D	No output.
	<----Right Answer

Q.32: What is the output?

```
class Program {
 static void main(String args[]){
  System.out.println("Namaskar");
 }
}
```

A	Runtime error.
B	Compiler error.
C	Namaskar.
D	No output.
	<----Right Answer

Q.33: What is the output?

```
class Program {
 void static main(String args[]){
  System.out.println("Namaskar");
 }
}
```

A	Namaskar.
B	Compiler error.
C	Runtime error.
D	No output.
	<----Right Answer

Q.34: "System.out.println()" method is part of ………….. class.

A	Printer.
B	PrintWriter.
C	PrintStream.
D	Print.
	<----Right Answer

Q.35: What is the output?

```
class Program {
 public void static main(String args[]){
  System.out.println("Namaskar");
 }
}
```

A	Compiler error.
B	Runtime error.
C	Namaskar.
D	Helloworld.
	<----Right Answer

Q.36: What is the output?

```
class Program {
 private static void main(String args[]){
  System.out.println("Namaskar");
 }
}
```

A	Compiler error.
B	Runtime error.
C	Namaskar.
D	Helloworld.
	<----Right Answer

Q.37: What is the output?

```
class Program {
 void main(String args[]){
  System.out.println("Namaskar");
 }
}
```

A	Namaskar.
B	No output.
C	Runtime error.
D	Compiler error.
	<----Right Answer

Q.38: .... is the default package in Java.

A	java.io
B	java.lang
C	java.net
D	java.data
B	**<----Right Answer**

Q.39: What is the output?	

class Program {
 protected void static main(String args[]){
  System.out.println("Namaskar");
 }
}	

A	Runtime error.
B	Compiler error.
C	Namaskar.
D	No output.
	<----Right Answer

Q.40: What is the output?	

class Program {
 private void static main(String args[]){
  System.out.println("Namaskar");
 }
}	

A	Compiler error.
B	Runtime error.
C	Namaskar.
D	Helloworld.
	<----Right Answer

Answers:

Q.No	Ans	Explanation
1	D	The valid extension of java program is .java .
2	A	Java program file extension is case sensitive.
3	A	Invalid file extension.
4	A	// is used for giving single line comments.
5	C	/* ... */ is used for giving multi line comments.
6	B	Invalid file extension.

7	A	Java program compiles to .class file.
8	B	Binary java code is also called as bytecode.
9	B	Extension of java file is .java .
10	C	Prg.java is a valid java file name.
11	C	main() method is the entry point in a java program.
12	A	Incorrect main method.
13	A	Correct main method public static void main(String ...a)
14	B	By computation the output is: HelloWorld.
15	B	By computation the output is: HelloWorld Ram,Hari.
16	D	By computation the output is: Namaskar :[Ljava.lang.String;@2a139a55.
17	D	By computation the output is: HelloWorld.
18	A	Correct signature is : public static void main(String args[]).
19	D	Insufficient command line argument.
20	A	System class belongs to java.lang package.
21	B	Incorrect main method signature.
22	B,C	Valid signatures are: public static void main(String[] args). public static void main(String args[]).
23	C	By computation the output is: HelloWorld.
24	B	By computation the output is: HelloWorld.
25	A	Incorrect signature of main method.
26	B	Main method is duplicating.
27	B	System.out is an object of PrintStream class.
28	A	By computation the result is 30.
29	A	Incorrect signature of main method.
30	A	Summation of string is invalid.
31	C	Incorrect main method signature.
32	A	Incorrect signature of main method.
33	B	Incorrect signature of main method.
34	C	println() method belongs to PrintStream class.
35	A	Incorrect signature of main method.

36	B	No valid main() method present.
37	C	No valid main() method present.
38	B	java.lang is the default package in Java.
39	B	No valid main() method signature in the program.
40	A	No valid main() signature in the program.

Chapter 4
HelloWorld Program - II

Q.1: How many classes can a Java program can have?	
A	1
B	2
C	4
D	None of the above.
	<----Right Answer

Q.2: The ".class" file has the same name as the class defined in the program.	
A	TRUE.
B	FALSE.
C	Sometimes.
D	None of the above.
	<----Right Answer

Q.3: How many entry point "main" methods can a class have?	
A	1
B	2
C	4
D	8
	<----Right Answer

Q.4: If a Java program has 4 classes then how many class files will be generated after compilation?	
A	2
B	1
C	4
D	8
	<----Right Answer

Q.5: Main method can be overloaded.	
A	True.
B	False.
	<----Right Answer

Q.6: What is the output?	

class Program {
     public static void main(String args[]) {
        System.out.println("Namaskar");
     }
     public static void main() {
 System.out.println ("Main() method");
     }
     public void main(String ar) {
System.out.println("String argument-main");
     }
}	

A	Namaskar.
B	Main() method.
C	String argument-main.
D	Runtime error.
	<----Right Answer

Q.7: What is the output?	

class Program {
     public static void main(String args[]) {
        System.out.println("Namaskar");
     }
     public static void main(String ... args) {
        System.out.println("Vanakkam");
     }
}	

A	Vanakkam.
B	Namaskar.
C	Runtime error.
D	Compiler error.
	<----Right Answer

Q.8: What is the output(When Test class is executed)?
class Program { public static void main(String args[]) {

```
        System.out.println("Program class - Main method");
 }

}

class Test {
        public static void main(String[] args) {
                System.out.println("Test class - Main method");
        }
}
```

A	Compiler error.
B	Runtime error.
C	Program class – Main method.
D	Test class – Main method.
	<----Right Answer

Q.9: Identify the invalid signature for main method which is an entry point in a class.

A	public static void main(String args[]).
B	public static void main(String[] args).
C	public static void main(String ...args).
D	public static void main(string[] args).
	<----Right Answer

Q.10: How many public classes can be created in a Java program?

A	1
B	2
C	Any number.
D	0
	<----Right Answer

Q.11: What is the output?

```
class Program {
        public static void main(String args[]) {
                System.out.println("Program Namaskar");
        }
        public static void main(String ... args) {
                System.out.println("Program Vanakkam");
        }
}
```

```
class Test {
        public static void main(String args[]) {
                System.out.println("Test Namaskar");
        }
        public static void main(String ... args) {
                System.out.println("Test Vanakkam");
        }
}
```

A	Runtime error.
B	Compiler error.
C	Program Namaskar.
D	Test Namaskar.
	<----Right Answer

Q.12: What is the output(When Test class is executed)?

```
class Program {
 public static void main(String args[] ) {
   System.out.println("Program class - Main method");
 }

}

class Test {
        static void main(String[] args) {
        System.out.println("Test class - Main method");
        }
}
```

A	Compiler error.
B	Program class – Main method.
C	Runtime error.
D	Test class – Main method.
	<----Right Answer

Q.13: The program name and public class should be same.

A	True.
B	False.
	<----Right Answer

Q.14: How many default scoped classes(Package level) can be created in a program?

A	1
B	2
C	0
D	Any number.
	<----Right Answer

Q.15: What is the output (The name of the Java program is MyPrg.java)?

```
// MyPrg.java
public class Prg {
 public static void main(String args[]) {
  System.out.println("Namaste Java");
 }
}
```

A	Namaste Java.
B	Runtime error.
C	Compiler error.
D	None of the above.
	<----Right Answer

Q.16: How many private classes can be created in a Java program?

A	0
B	2
C	1
D	Any number
	<----Right Answer

Q.17: What is the output?

```
public private class Prg {
 public static void main(String args[]) {
  System.out.println("Namaste Java");
 }
}
```

A	Runtime error.
B	Namaste Java.
C	Compiler error.
D	None of the above.
	<----Right Answer

Q.18: How many protected classes can be created in a Java program?

A	1
B	2
C	0
D	Any number.
	<----Right Answer

Q.19: What is the output (The name of the java Program is 44.java)?

```
// 44.java
class Prg {
 public static void main(String args[]) {
  System.out.println("Namaste Java");
 }
}
```

A	Compiler error.
B	Runtime error.
C	Namaste Java.
D	None of the above.
	<----Right Answer

Q.20: What is the output (The name of the Java program is MyPrg.java)?

```
// MyPrg.java
protected class Prg {
 public static void main(String args[]) {
  System.out.println("Namaste Java");
 }
}
```

A	Runtime error.
B	Compiler error.
C	Namaste Java.
D	None of the above.
	<----Right Answer

Q.21: What is the output (The name of the Java program is MyPrg.java)?

```
// MyPrg.java
private class Prg {
 public static void main(String args[]) {
  System.out.println("Namaste Java");
 }
```

}	
A	Namaste Java.
B	Runtime error.
C	Compiler error.
D	None of the above.
	<----Right Answer

Q.22: What is the output?

```
public class Prg {
 public static void main(String args[]) {
  System.out.println("Namaste Java");
 }
}
```

A	Namaste Java.
B	Runtime error.
C	Compiler error.
D	None of the above.
	<----Right Answer

Q.23: What is the output when Prg2 class is executed (The name of the Java program is Prg.java)?

```
//Prg.java
public class Prg {
 public static void main(String args[]) {
  System.out.println("Namaste Java");
 }
}

public class Prg2 {
 public static void main(String args[]) {
  System.out.println("Namaste Java2");
 }
}
```

A	Compiler error.
B	Namaste Java.
C	Runtime error.
D	Namaste Java2.
	<----Right Answer

Q.24: What is the output (The name of the Java program is MyPrg.java)?

```
class Prg {
```

```
  public static void main(String args[]) {
   System.out.println("Namaste Java");
  }
 }
```

A	Namaste Java.
B	Compiler error.
C	Runtime error.
D	None of the above.
	<----Right Answer

Q.25: What is the output (The name of the Java program is 44.java)?

```
class 44 {
 public static void main(String args[]) {
  System.out.println("Namaste Java");
 }
}
```

A	Namaste Java.
B	Compiler error.
C	Runtime error.
D	None of the above.
	<----Right Answer

Q.26: What is the output?

```
public class Prg {
 public static void main(String args[]) {
  System.out.println("Namaste Java");
   public static void main(String args[]) {
        System.out.println("Inner Namaste Java");
  }
 }
}
```

A	Namaste Java.
B	Namaste Java
	Inner Namaste Java.
C	Compiler error.
D	Runtime error.
	<----Right Answer

Q.27: JIT stands for ....

A	Just In Time Compilation.
B	Java In Time Compilation.
C	Java Information Technology.
D	Java Input Technique.
	<----Right Answer

Q.28: JIT is performed by ....

A	Compiler.
B	Interpreter.
C	Bytecode reader.
D	Security Manager.
	<----Right Answer

Q.29: .... Activity happens at runtime.

A	Compilation.
B	JIT.
C	Coding.
D	None of the above.
	<----Right Answer

Q.30:The process of conversion of Bytecode to Native code is called as ....

A	Compilation.
B	Garbage collection.
C	JIT.
D	Testing.
	<----Right Answer

Q.31: Binary code of Java is called as ....

A	Source code.
B	IL code.
C	Byte code.
D	Native code.
	<----Right Answer

Q.32: The process of converting source code to bytecode is called as ......

A	Compilation.
B	Interpretation.
C	JIT.
D	None of the above.
	<----Right Answer

Q.33: FileOutputStream class belongs to .... package.

A	java.lang
B	java.io
C	java.net
D	None of the above
	<----Right Answer

Q.34: Java byte code targets .... operating system.

A	Windows.
B	Linux.
C	Mac OS.
D	None of the above.
	<----Right Answer

Q.35: Java bytecode is saved as .... file.

A	.java
B	.class
C	.exe
D	.byc
	<----Right Answer

Q.36: What is the output?

```
import java.io.*;
class Program {
 public static void main(String args[]) {
      FileOutputStream obj = new FileOutputStream(FileDescriptor.out);
      PrintStream obj2 = new PrintStream(obj);
      obj2.println("Alternative Namaste Java");
 }
```

}	
A	Namaste Java.
B	Alternative Namaste Java.
C	Compiler error.
D	Runtime error.
	<----Right Answer

Q.37: .... Identifies the output stream.

A	FileDescriptor.out
B	FileDescriptor.stdout
C	FileDescriptor.vdu
D	FileDescriptor.std
	<----Right Answer

Q.38: Identify the correct statement

A	Bytecode targets Windows OS.
B	Bytecode targets Linux OS.
C	Bytecode targets JVM.
D	Bytecode targets Ubuntu.
	<----Right Answer

Q.39: Identify the correct statement.

A	Conversion of Native code to Bytecode is called as JIT.
B	Conversion of Bytecode to Source code is called compilation.
C	Conversion of Bytecode to Native code is called Garbage collection.
D	Conversion of Source code to Bytecode is called as Compilation.
	<----Right Answer

Q.40: PrintStream class belongs to .... Package.

A	java.io
B	java.lang
C	java.net
D	java.data
	<----Right Answer

Q.41: Bytecode targets	
A	Java compiler.
B	JVM.
C	Windows OS.
D	Linux OS.
	<----**Right Answer**

Answers:

Q.No	Ans	Explanation
1	D	A Java program can have any number of classes.
2	A	.class file has the same name as the class in code.
3	A	A class can have only one entry point.
4	C	Every class will compile to .class file.
5	A	Main method can be overloaded.
6	A	By computation the output is Namaskar.
7	D	A class can have only one entry point.
8	D	By computation the output is Test class – Main method.
9	D	It is invalid signature.
10	A	A program can only have one public class.
11	B	A class can have only one entry point.
12	C	Test class does not have entry point.
13	A	Program name and public class name are same.
14	D	There can be any number of default scoped classes in a program.
15	C	Program name and public class names are same.
16	A	Classes cannot be private
17	C	Class cannot be private.
18	C	Classes cannot be protected.
19	C	By computation the output is Namaste Java.
20	B	Class cannot be protected.
21	C	Class cannot be private.
22	A	By computation the output is Namaste Java.

23	A	There can only be one public class.
24	A	By computation the output is Namaste Java.
25	B	Class name cannot be numeric.
26	C	Methods cannot be nested.
27	A	JIT stands for Just In Time Compilation.
28	B	JIT is performed by interpreter.
29	B	JIT happens at runtime.
30	C	Converting bytecode to native code is called as JIT
31	C	Binary code of Java is called as bytecode.
32	A	Conversion of source code to bytecode is called as compilation.
33	B	FileOutputStream belongs to java.io package.
34	D	Java bytecode does not target any OS.
35	B	Java bytecode is saved in .class file.
36	B	By computation the output is Alternative Namaste Java.
37	A	FileDescriptor.out refers to output stream.
38	C	Bytecode only targets the OS.
39	D	Conversion of Source code to Bytecode is called as Compilation.
40	A	PrintStream class belongs to java.io package.
41	B	Bytecode targets JVM.

Chapter 5
Data Types-I

Q.1: Which of the following is not a primitive?	
A	int.
B	byte.
C	char.
D	number.
	<----Right Answer

Q.2: What is the size of char data type (in bytes)?	
A	1
B	2
C	4
D	8
	<----Right Answer

Q.3: How much memory does short data type consume (in bytes)?	
A	4
B	2
C	1
D	8
	<----Right Answer

Q.4: Which of the following is not a primitive?	
A	long.
B	double.
C	boolean.
D	String
	<----Right Answer

Q.5: What is the size of a byte variable (in bytes)	
A	4

B	1
C	8
D	2
	<----Right Answer

| Q.6: How much memory does long variable take (in bytes)? |
A	2
B	4
C	8
D	16
	<----Right Answer

| Q.7: .... Is the default integer type. |
A	int.
B	byte.
C	long.
D	number.
	<----Right Answer

| Q.8: .... Is the default floating type. |
A	short.
B	float.
C	double.
D	single.
	<----Right Answer

| Q.9: Which of the following is not a primitive? |
A	short.
B	float.
C	single.
D	double.
	<----Right Answer

| Q.10: How much memory does int data type take (in bytes)? |

A	2
B	8
C	16
D	4
	<----Right Answer

Q.11: Which of the following type is signed?

A	byte.
B	int.
C	double.
D	All of the above.
	<----Right Answer

Q.12: What is the default value of a Boolean variable?

A	true.
B	false.
C	Null.
D	Junk.
	<----Right Answer

Q.13: What is the output?

```
class Program {
 public static void show() {
  byte b=-128;
  System.out.println("Byte value :"+b);
 }
 public static void main(String args[]){
   show();
 }
}
```

A	-128.
B	Compiler error.
C	Runtime error.
D	0.
	<----Right Answer

Q.14: Which of the following is not a Primitive?

A	Object.

B	int.
C	boolean.
D	char.
	<----Right Answer

Q.15: What is the output?

```
class Program {
 public static void show() {
  boolean b;
  System.out.println("Boolean value :"+b);
 }
 public static void main(String args[]){
   show();
 }
}
```

A	false.
B	true.
C	Compiler error.
D	Runtime error.
	<----Right Answer

Q.16: What is the output?

```
class Program {
 public static void show() {
  byte b=-129;
  System.out.println("Byte value :"+b);
 }
 public static void main(String args[]){
   show();
 }
}
```

A	-129.
B	Runtime error.
C	Compiler error.
D	1.
	<----Right Answer

Q.17: Identify the invalid data type?

A	float.
B	double.
C	number.

D	byte.
	<----Right Answer

Q.18: Identify the reference data type?

A	int.
B	long.
C	String.
D	Object.
	<----Right Answer

Q.19: What is the output?

```
class Program {
 public static void show() {
  float f=12.23;
  System.out.println("Float value :"+f);
 }
 public static void main(String args[]){
   show();
 }
}
```

A	12.23
B	12
C	Runtime error.
D	Compiler error.
	<----Right Answer

Q.20: What is the output?

```
class Program {
 public static void show() {
  double f=12.23;
  System.out.println("Double value :"+f);
 }
 public static void main(String args[]){
   show();
 }
}
```

A	12.23
B	12
C	Compiler error.
D	Runtime error.
	<----Right Answer

Q.21: What is the output?

```
class Program {
 public static void show() {
  float f=12.23f;
  int i = 20;
  i = i*f;
  System.out.println("Result:"+i);
 }
 public static void main(String args[]){
   show();
 }
}
```

A	244
B	200
C	Compiler error.
D	Runtime error.
	<----Right Answer

Q.22: What is the output?

```
class Program {
 public static void show() {
  byte b =10;
  int i = 20;
  i = i*b;
  System.out.println("Result:"+i);
 }
 public static void main(String args[]){
   show();
 }
}
```

A	200
B	10
C	Compiler error.
D	Runtime error.
	<----Right Answer

Q.23: What is the output?

```
class Program {
 public static void show() {
  byte b =10;
  int i = 20;
```

```
  b = i*b;
  System.out.println("Result:"+b);
 }
 public static void main(String args[]){
   show();
 }
}
```

A	244
B	200
C	Compiler error.
D	Runtime error.
	<----Right Answer

Q.24: What is the output?

```
class Program {
 public static void show() {
  float f =10.13;
  int i = 20;
  f = i*f;
  System.out.println("Result:"+f);
 }
 public static void main(String args[]){
   show();
 }
}
```

A	Runtime error.
B	Compiler error.
C	202
D	202.6
	<----Right Answer

Q.25: What is the output?

```
class Program {
 public static void show() {
  float f=12.23f;
  int i = 20;
  f = i*f;
  System.out.println("Result:"+f);
 }
 public static void main(String args[]){
   show();
 }
}
```

A	244.5599
B	12.23
C	Runtime error.
D	Compiler error.
	<----Right Answer

Q.26: What is the output?

```
class Program {
 public static void show() {
  short sh;
  System.out.println("Short value :"+sh);
 }
 public static void main(String args[]){
   show();
 }
}
```

A	0.
B	Null.
C	Compiler error.
D	Runtime error.
	<----Right Answer

Q.27: What is the output?

```
class Program {
 public static void mixedOps() {
  float f = 10.10f;
  int j =10;
  j = (int) f * j;
  System.out.println(j);
 }
 public static void main(String args[]){
        mixedOps();
 }
}
```

A	Runtime error.
B	Compiler error.
C	100
D	100.00
	<----Right Answer

Q.28: What is the default value of long variable?

A	Junk.
B	Null.
C	0.
D	-1.
	<----Right Answer

Q.29: What is the output?

```
class Program {
 public static void mixedOps() {
  float f = 2.2;
  double d =3.3;
  f = f * d;
  System.out.println("Result :" + f);
 }
 public static void main(String args[]){
      mixedOps();
 }
}
```

A	6.6
B	7.26
C	Compiler error.
D	Runtime error.
	<----Right Answer

Q.30: What is the output?

```
class Program {
 public static void mixedOps() {
  float f = 2.2f;
  double d =3.3d;
  d = f * d;
  System.out.println("Result :" + d);
 }
 public static void main(String args[]){
      mixedOps();
 }
}
```

A	Compiler error.
B	Runtime error.
C	7.26
D	6.6
	<----Right Answer

Q.31: What is the output?

```
class Program {
 public static void mixedOps() {
  float f = 2.2f;
  double d =3.3d;
  f = f * d;
  System.out.println(f);
 }
 public static void main(String args[]){
       mixedOps();
 }
}
```

A	7.26
B	6.6
C	Compiler error.
D	Runtime error.
	<----Right Answer

Q.32: What is the output?

```
class Program {
 public static void mixedOps() {
  boolean b = true;
  int i=10;
  i= (int)b *i;
  System.out.println("Result :" + i);
 }
 public static void main(String args[]){
       mixedOps();
 }
}
```

A	Runtime error.
B	Compiler error.
C	10.
D	11.
	<----Right Answer

Q.33: What is the output?

```
class Program {
 public static void mixedOps() {
  boolean b = true;
  int i=10;
  b= (boolean)i*b;
  System.out.println("Result :" + b);
```

```
}
public static void main(String args[]){
     mixedOps();
}
}
```

A	true.
B	false.
C	Compiler error.
D	Runtime error.
	<----Right Answer

Q.34: Which data type size is 2 bytes?

A	char.
B	short.
C	int.
D	long.
	<----Right Answer

Q.35: Which data type size is 1 byte?

A	boolean.
B	byte.
C	int.
D	char.
	<----Right Answer

Q.36: Which data type size is dependent on JVM?

A	long.
B	double.
C	float.
D	boolean.
	<----Right Answer

Q.37: Which data type occupies 8 bytes?

A	short int.
B	int.
C	long int.
D	long.

| | | <----**Right Answer** |

Q.38: Which data type occupies 4 bytes?	
A	int.
B	double.
C	long.
D	float.
	<----**Right Answer**

Q.39: What is the output?	

```
class Program {
 public static void mixedOps() {
  float f = 10.10f;
  int j =10;
  f = (int) f * j;
  System.out.println("Result :" + f);
 }
 public static void main(String args[]){
        mixedOps();
 }
}
```

A	100
B	100.0
C	Compiler error.
D	Runtime error.
	<----**Right Answer**

Q.40: What is the output?	

```
class Program {
 public static void mixedOps() {
  float f = 10.10f;
  int j =10;
  f = (float) f * j;
  System.out.println("Result :" + f);
 }
 public static void main(String args[]){
        mixedOps();
 }
}
```

A	100
B	101

C	100.0
D	101.0
	<----Right Answer

Q.41: Identify the correct statement	
A	boolean variable can be casted to int.
B	int variable can be casted to boolean.
C	float variable can be casted to boolean.
D	float variable can be casted to int.
	<----Right Answer

Q.42:Which data types occupies 8 bytes?	
A	float.
B	long float.
C	double.
D	long.
	<----Right Answer

Answers:

Q.No	Ans	Explanation
1	D	number is not a primitive in Java.
2	B	char type occupies 2 bytes.
3	B	short type occupies 2 bytesc
4	D	String is not a primitive.
5	B	byte data type occupies 1 byte.
6	C	long datatype occupies 8 bytes.
7	A	int is the default integer type.
8	C	double is the default floating type.
9	C	single is not a primitive in Java.
10	D	int datatype takes 4 bytes.
11	D	byte,int and double are signed datatypes.

12	B	Default value of boolean datatype is false.
13	A	By computation the result is -128.
14	A	Object is not a primitive.
15	C	Variable is not initialized.
16	C	Byte value is invalid.
17	C	Number is the invalid type.
18	C,D	String and Object are reference type.
19	D	Invalid value in float type. Suffix 'f' with the value.
20	A	By computation the result is 12.23 .
21	C	Invalid expression.
22	A	By computation the result is 200.
23	C	Invalid expression.
24	B	Invalid expression.
25	A	By computation the result is 244.5599 .
26	C	Variable not initialized.
27	C	By computation the result is 100.
28	C	Default value for long is 0.
29	C	Invalid expression.
30	C	By computation the result is 7.26 .
31	C	Invalid expression.
32	B	Invalid expression.
33	C	Invalid expression.
34	A,B	char & short types occupy 2 bytes.
35	B	byte occupies 1 byte.
36	D	boolean variable size is dependent in the JVM.
37	D	Long type occupies 8 bytes.
38	A,D	Int & float occupies 4 bytes each.
39	B	By computation the result is 100.0
40	D	By computation the result is 101.
41	D	Float variable can be casted to int.
42	C,D	double and long variables occupy 8 bytes each.

Chapter 6
Data Types - II

Q.1: Which of the following is a signed type?	
A	char.
B	boolean.
C	float.
D	single.
	<----Right Answer

Q.2: Which of the following data type occupies the highest memory?	
A	long.
B	double.
C	long int.
D	float.
	<----Right Answer

Q.3: Which of the following data type occupies the least memory?	
A	int.
B	short.
C	char.
D	float.
	<----Right Answer

Q.4: Which of the following type is immutable?	
A	char.
B	boolean.
C	String.
D	float.
	<----Right Answer

Q.5: Identify non-reference data types?	

A	float.
B	long.
C	String.
D	Object.
	<----Right Answer

Q.6: How much memory does float data type occupy?

A	2
B	4
C	8
D	16
	<----Right Answer

Q.7: How much memory does double data type occupy?

A	16
B	2
C	8
D	4
	<----Right Answer

Q.8: How much memory does Boolean data type occupy?

A	1
B	2
C	4
D	Depends on JVM.
	<----Right Answer

Q.9: What is the output?

```
class Program {
  boolean b;
 public void defValue() {
  System.out.println(b);
 }

 public static void main(String args[]) {
  Program obj = new Program();
  obj.defValue();
```

	`}`
	`}`
A	true.
B	false.
C	Compiler error.
D	Runtime error.
	<----Right Answer

Q.10: What is the output?

```
class Program {
 char c;
 public void defValue() {
  System.out.println("Result:" + c);
 }

 public static void main(String args[]) {
  Program obj = new Program();
  obj.defValue();
 }
}
```

A	Result:
B	Compiler error.
C	Runtime error.
D	None of the above.
	<----Right Answer

Q.11: Identify the hexadecimal literal.

A	int i=0x1234;
B	int i=10;
C	int j=0123;
D	int i=7;
	<----Right Answer

Q.12: What is the output?

```
class Program {
 public static void defValue() {
  int i=012;
  System.out.println(i);
 }

 public static void main(String args[]) {
```

```
  defValue();
 }
}
```

A	Compiler error.
B	Runtime error.
C	12
D	10
	<----Right Answer

Q.13: What is the output?

```
class Program {
 public static void defValue() {
  int i=0xA;
  System.out.println(i);
 }

 public static void main(String args[]) {
  defValue();
 }
}
```

A	Compiler error.
B	Runtime error.
C	12
D	10
	<----Right Answer

Q.14: What is the output?

```
class Program {
 public static void defValue() {
  long l=34343L;
  System.out.println("Result:" + l);
 }

 public static void main(String args[]) {
  defValue();
 }
}
```

A	34343
B	34343L
C	Compiler error.
D	Runtime error.
	<----Right Answer

Q.15: What is the output?

```
class Program {
 public void defValue() {
  boolean b;
  System.out.println(b);
 }

 public static void main(String args[]) {
  Program obj = new Program();
  obj.defValue();
 }
}
```

A	Compiler error.
B	Runtime error.
C	True.
D	False.
	<----Right Answer

Q.16: What is the output?

```
class Program {
 public static void defValue() {
  int i=0xfg;
  System.out.println(i);
 }

 public static void main(String args[]) {
  defValue();
 }
}
```

A	16
B	18
C	Runtime error.
D	Compiler error.
	<----Right Answer

Q.17: What is the output?

```
class Program {
 public static void defValue() {
  int i=0xf;
  System.out.println(i);
 }

 public static void main(String args[]) {
```

```
  defValue();
 }
}
```

A	Runtime error.
B	12
C	15
D	10
	<----Right Answer

Q.18: What is the output?

```
class Program {
 public void defValue() {
  char c;
  System.out.println(c);
 }

 public static void main(String args[]) {
  Program obj = new Program();
  obj.defValue();
 }
}
```

A	Result:
B	Compiler error.
C	Data error.
D	Runtime error.
	<----Right Answer

Q.19: What is the output?

```
class Program {
 public static void defValue() {
  int i=0f1;
  System.out.println(i);
 }

 public static void main(String args[]) {
  defValue();
 }
}
```

A	15
B	12
C	Compiler error.
D	Runtime error.
	<----Right Answer

Q.20: Identify the octal literal.	
A	int i=0121;
B	int i=o897;
C	int i=0X123;
D	int i=0x124;
	<----Right Answer

Q.21: What is the output?

```
class Program {
 public static void defValue() {
  int a= 010;
  int b= 011;
  a = a*b;
  System.out.println(a);
 }

 public static void main(String args[]) {
  defValue();
 }
}
```

A	64
B	72
C	81
D	Compiler error.
	<----Right Answer

Q.22: What is the output?

```
class Program {
 public static void defValue() {
  int a= 0xa;
  int b=0xb;
  a=a*b;
  System.out.println(a);
 }

 public static void main(String args[]) {
  defValue();
 }
}
```

A	122
B	110

C	90
D	Compiler error.
	<----Right Answer

Q.23: What is the output?

```
class Program {
 public static void defValue() {
  int a= 0xg;
  int b=0xa;
  a=a*b;
  System.out.println(a);
 }

 public static void main(String args[]) {
  defValue();
 }
}
```

A	150
B	160
C	170
D	Compiler error.
	<----Right Answer

Q.24: What is the output?

```
class Program {
 public static void defValue() {
  int a= 30l;
  int b=50;
  a=a*b;
  System.out.println(a);
 }

 public static void main(String args[]) {
  defValue();
 }
}
```

A	1500
B	Compiler error.
C	Runtime error.
D	30
	<----Right Answer

Q.25: What is the output?

```
class Program {
 public static void defValue() {
  int a= 08;
  System.out.println(a);
 }

 public static void main(String args[]) {
  defValue();
 }
}
```

A	Compiler error.
B	Runtime error.
C	8
D	9
	<----Right Answer

Q.26: What is the output?

```
class Program {
 public static void defValue() {
  int a= 010;
  System.out.println(a);
 }

 public static void main(String args[]) {
  defValue();
 }
}
```

A	Runtime error.
B	Compiler error.
C	9
D	8
	<----Right Answer

Q.27: What is the output?

```
class Program {
 public static void defValue() {
  String str=null;
  System.out.println(str);
 }

 public static void main(String args[]) {
  defValue();
```

	} }	
A	Null.	
B	Compiler error.	
C	Runtime error.	
D	None of the above.	
	<----Right Answer	

Q.28: What is the output?

```
class Program {
 public static void defValue() {
  char c=null;
  System.out.println(c);
 }

 public static void main(String args[]) {
  defValue();
 }
}
```

A	Runtime error.
B	Compiler error.
C	Null.
D	None of the above.
	<----Right Answer

Q.29: What is the output?

```
class Program {
 public static void defValue() {
  boolean b=null;
  System.out.println(b);
 }

 public static void main(String args[]) {
  defValue();
 }
}
```

A	Null.
B	Compiler error.
C	Runtime error.
D	None of the above.
	<----Right Answer

Q.30: How to create constant variable?

A	const keyword.
B	constant keyword.
C	final keyword.
D	def keyword.
	<----Right Answer

Q.31: How to insert new line in text?

A	\nl.
B	\n.
C	\b.
D	\t.
	<----Right Answer

Q.32: How to insert tab in text?

A	\tab.
B	\t.
C	\nt.
D	\tt.
	<----Right Answer

Q.33: How to insert backslash in text?

A	\b.
B	\bb.
C	\\.
D	\nb.
	<----Right Answer

Q.34: What is the output?

```
class Program {
 public static void defValue() {
  int a= 09;
  System.out.println(a);
 }

 public static void main(String args[]) {
  defValue();
```

	}
	}
A	9
B	Compiler error.
C	Runtime error.
D	8
	<----Right Answer

Q.35: How to insert backspace in text?

A	\\.
B	\bb.
C	\b.
D	\back.
	<----Right Answer

Q.36: How to insert double quote in text?

A	\dq.
B	\".
C	\'.
D	\dd.
	<----Right Answer

Q.37: Identify the invalid escape sequence?

A	\b.
B	\n.
C	\r.
D	\q.
	<----Right Answer

Q.38: Identify the invalid escape sequence?

A	\'.
B	\".
C	\%.
D	\\.
	<----Right Answer

Q.39: What is the output?

```
class Program {
 public static void defValue() {
  final float f=10.10f;
  f=20.20f;
  System.out.println(f);
 }

 public static void main(String args[]) {
  defValue();
 }
}
```

A	10.10
B	20.20
C	Compiler error.
D	Runtime error.
	<----Right Answer

Q.40: What is the output?

```
class Program {
 public static void defValue() {
  float f=null;
  System.out.println(f);
 }

 public static void main(String args[]) {
  defValue();
 }
}
```

A	Runtime error.
B	Null.
C	Compiler error.
D	None of the above.
	<----Right Answer

Q.41: What is the output?

```
class Program {
 public static void defValue() {
  int a= 09;
  int b=08;
  a=a*b;
  System.out.println(a);
 }
```

```
public static void main(String args[]) {
 defValue();
 }
}
```

A	Runtime error.
B	72
C	Compiler error.
D	81
	<----Right Answer

Q.42: How to give single quote in text?
A	\"
B	\\'
C	\'
D	\q
	<----Right Answer

Answers:

Q.No	Ans	Explanation
1	C	Float is signed typed.
2	A,B	long and double occupy 8 bytes each.
3	B,C	short and char occupy 2 bytes each.
4	C	String is immutable.
5	A,B	float and long are primitivites.
6	B	float type occupies 4 bytes.
7	C	double type occupies 8 bytes.
8	D	Size of Boolean type depends on JVM.
9	B	By computation the result is true.
10	A	By computation the result is 'Result:' .
11	A	0x1234 is the hexadecimal literal.
12	D	By computation the result is 10.
13	C	By computation the result is 12.
14	A	By computation the result is 34343.

15	A	Boolean variable is not initialized.
16	D	Invalid hexadecimal number.
17	C	By computation the result is 15.
18	B	Char variable is not initialized.
19	C	Invalid octal number.
20	A	0121 is the octal number.
21	B	By computation the result is 72.
22	B	By computation the result is 110.
23	D	Invalid hexadecimal number.
24	B	Invalid integer number.
25	A	Invalid octal number.
26	D	By computation the result is 8.
27	A	By computation the result is null.
28	B	Primitives cannot be null.
29	B	Primitives cannot be null.
30	C	final keyword is used for decalring constants.
31	B	'\n' is used for new line escape sequence.
32	B	'\t' is used for giving tab.
33	C	'\\' is used for inserting backslash.
34	B	Invalid octal number.
35	C	'\b' is used for adding backspace.
36	B	\" is used for giving double quotes.
37	D	\q is invalid escape sequence.
38	C	\% is invalid escape sequence.
39	C	Final variable cannot be changed.
40	C	Primitives cannot be null.
41	C	Invalid octal numbers
42	C	\' is the single quote

Chapter 7
String Operations

Q.1: Which of the following data types do not support immutability?	
A	int.
B	float.
C	double.
D	All of the above.
	<----Right Answer

Q.2: Which of the following types have support for immutability?	
A	String.
B	string.
C	Stringbuilder.
D	char.
	<----Right Answer

Q.3: '==' operator(string) is used for .... comparison.	
A	Value.
B	Reference.
C	Case sensitive value.
D	None of the above.
	<----Right Answer

Q.4: Which of the following is a reference type?	
A	boolean.
B	char.
C	String.
D	byte.
	<----Right Answer

Q.5: String type variable is created on .... Memory.	
A	Stack.

B	Heap.
C	Near.
D	Far.
	<----Right Answer

Q.6: Boolean type variable is created on ....   Memory.

A	Heap.
B	Stack.
C	Extended.
D	Near.
	<----Right Answer

Q.7: Which method is used for concatenating two strings?

A	concatenate().
B	concat().
C	add().
D	merge().
	<----Right Answer

Q.8: How to perform case sensitive comparison between two strings?

A	equals().
B	same().
C	==.
D	compare().
	<----Right Answer

Q.9: How to compare two strings by reference?

A	#
B	==
C	equals().
D	compare().
	<----Right Answer

Q.10: How to perform case insensitive comparison of two strings?

A	equalsIgnoreCase().
B	compareIgnoreCase().
C	eqIgnoreCase().
D	eqCompareCase().
	<----Right Answer

Q.11: String class belongs to .... package	
A	java.io
B	java.lang
C	java.str
D	java.net
	<----Right Answer

Q.12:............... Method is used for adding string at the end of a StringBuilder object.	
A	add().
B	append().
C	insert().
D	merge().
	<----Right Answer

Q.13: .... Method is used for adding string in between a StringBuilder object.	
A	merge().
B	append().
C	insert().
D	add().
	<----Right Answer

Q.14: StringBuilder class belongs to .... Package.	
A	java.lang
B	java.net
C	java.str
D	java.io
	<----Right Answer

Q.15: Which of the following is mutable?	
A	string.
B	String.
C	StringBuilder.
D	StrBuilder.
	<----Right Answer

Q.16: Which of the following is an invalid types?	
A	Str.
B	string.
C	StringBuilder.
D	String.
	<----Right Answer

Q.17: .... Is used for value comparison of 2 strings.	
A	equals() method.
B	== operator.
C	=== operator.
D	equalsIgnoreCase() method.
	<----Right Answer

Q.18: StringBuilder object occupies .... Memory.	
A	Stack.
B	Heap.
C	Extended.
D	Far.
	<----Right Answer

Q.19: Which of the following objects are liable for garbage collection.	
A	boolean.
B	String.
C	char.
D	StringBuilder.
	<----Right Answer

Q.20: .... Method is used for deleting string from a StringBuilder object.	
A	remove().
B	delete().
C	purge().
D	zap().
	<----Right Answer

Q.21: What is the output?	

class Program {
     static void strOps() {
         String str = "Namaste";
         String str2 = "namaste";
         System.out.println(str2.equalsIgnoreCase(str));
     }
 	
     public static void main(String args[]) {
         strOps();
     }
}	

A	false.
B	true.
C	Compiler error.
D	Runtime error.
	<----Right Answer

Q.22: What is the output?	

class Program {
     static void strOps() {
   String s = "Namaste";
   s.concat(" Java");
   System.out.println(s);
   }
 	
     public static void main(String args[]){
   strOps();
   }
}	

A	Namaste Java.
B	Namaste.
C	Java.
D	NamasteJava.

Q.23: What is the output?
| ```
class Program {
        static void strOps() {
                String str = "Namaste";
                String str2 = "namaste";
                System.out.println(str2.equals(str));
        }

        public static void main(String args[]) {
                strOps();
        }
}
``` |

A	true.
B	false.
C	Compiler error.
D	Runtime error.
	<----Right Answer

Q.24: What is the output?
| ```
class Program {
        static void strOps() {
          String s = "Namaste";
          s=s.concat(" Java");
          System.out.println(s);
        }

        public static void main(String args[]){
          strOps();
        }
}
``` |

A	Java.
B	Namaste.
C	Namaste Java.
D	NamasteJava.
	<----Right Answer

Q.25: What is the output?
| ```
class Program {
        static void strOps() {
                String str = "Namaste";
``` |
```

```
                String str2 = "namaste";
                System.out.println(str2.equalsCase(str));
        }

        public static void main(String args[]) {
                strOps();
        }
}
```

A	Compiler error.
B	Runtime error.
C	true.
D	false.
	<----Right Answer

Q.26: What is the output?
| ```
class Program {
        static void strOps() {
                String str = "Namaste";
                String str2 = "namaste";
                System.out.println(str==str2);
        }
        public static void main(String args[]) {
                strOps();
        }
}
``` |

A	true.
B	false.
C	Compiler error.
D	Runtime error.
	<----Right Answer

Q.27: What is the output?
| ```
class Program {
        static void strOps() {
                String str = "Namaste";
                String str2 = str;
                System.out.println(str==str2);
        }
        public static void main(String args[]) {
                strOps();
        }
}
``` |

| A | true. |

B	false.
C	Compiler error.
D	Runtime error.
	<----Right Answer

Q.28: What is the output?

```
class Program {
    public static void main(String[] args) {
    StringBuilder str = new StringBuilder("Namaste");
    str.append(" Java");
    System.out.println(str);
    }
}
```

A	Namaste Java.
B	Namaste.
C	Java.
D	NamasteJava.
	<----Right Answer

Q.29: What is the output?

```
class Program {
    public static void main(String[] args) {
    StringBuilder str = new StringBuilder("Namaste");
    str.insert(5," Vanakkam");
    System.out.println(str);
    }
}
```

A	Namas Vanakkamt.
B	NamasVanakkamte.
C	Namas Vanakkamte.
D	Namas Vankamte.
	<----Right Answer

Q.30: What is the output

```
class Program {
    public static void main(String[] args) {
    StringBuilder str = new   StringBuilder("Namaste");
    str.delete(2,5);
    System.out.println(str);
```

	}
}	
A	Nate.
B	Na.
C	Nat.
D	N.
	<----Right Answer

Answers:

Q.No	Ans	Explanation
1	D	Primitives are not immutable.
2	A	String is immutable.
3	B	"==" operator is used for reference comparison.
4	C	String is a reference type.
5	B	String variable goes on heap.
6	B	Boolean variable goes on stack.
7	B	concat() method is used for concatenating 2 strings.
8	A	equals() method is used for case sensitive comparison between 2 strings.
9	B	== operator is used for reference comparison between 2 strings.
10	A	Case insensitive comparison is done using equalsIgnoreCase() method.
11	B	String class belongs to java.lang package.
12	B	append() method is used for adding string at the end of StringBuilder object.
13	C	insert() method is used for adding string in between the StringBuilder object.
14	A	StringBuilder class belongs to java.lang package.
15	C	StringBuilder object is mutable.
16	A,B	Str and string are invalid types.
17	A,D	equals() and equalsIgnoreCase() methods are used for string comparison.
18	B	StringBuilder object goes on heap.
19	B,D	String and StringBuilder objects are liable for garbage collection.

20	A	remove() method is used for deleting string from StringBuilder object.
21	B	By computation the result is true.
22	B	By computation the result is Namaste.
23	B	By computation the result is false.
24	C	By computation the result is Namaste Java.
25	A	Code is invalid.
26	B	By computation the result is false.
27	A	By computation the result is true.
28	A	By computation the result is Namaste Java.
29	C	By computation the result is Namas Vanakkamte.
30	A	By computation the result is Nate.

Chapter 8
Wrapper Classes

Q.1: Identify the wrapper class for String type.	
A	Str.
B	StrBuilder.
C	StringBuilder.
D	None of the above.
	<----Right Answer

Q.2: Identify the wrapper class for Object type.	
A	Obj.
B	CObject.
C	Base.
D	None of the above.
	<----Right Answer

Q.3: Identify the wrapper class for boolean type.	
A	Bool.
B	Boolean.
C	BoolClass.
D	None of the above.
	<----Right Answer

Q.4: Identify the wrapper class for double type.	
A	Double.
B	Dbl.
C	Single.
D	None of the above.
	<----Right Answer

Q.5: Identify the wrapper class for char type.	

A	Char.
B	Text.
C	Character.
D	String.
	<----Right Answer

Q.6: Identify the wrapper class for float type.

A	Single.
B	Flt.
C	Floating.
D	Float.
	<----Right Answer

Q.7: Identify the wrapper class for byte type.

A	Byte.
B	Byt.
C	SingleByte.
D	None of the above.
	<----Right Answer

Q.8: Identify the wrapper class for long type.

A	Large.
B	BigNumber.
C	Number.
D	Long.
	<----Right Answer

Q.9: Identify the wrapper class for int type.

A	Number.
B	Integer.
C	Num.
D	Int.
	<----Right Answer

Q.10: Identify the wrapper class for short type

A	Number.
B	Sht.
C	Short.
D	None of the above.
	<----Right Answer

Q.11: What is unboxing?

A	Converting primitive type to wrapper class.
B	Converting wrapper class to primitive type.
C	Converting primitive to object.
D	Converting object to primitive.
	<----Right Answer

Q.12: What is the output?

```
class Program {
        static void wrapperOps() {
                int i=10;
                Short sh = i;
                System.out.println(sh);
        }

        public static void main(String args[]) {
        wrapperOps();
        }
}
```

A	10.
B	Compiler error.
C	11.
D	Runtime error.
	<----Right Answer

Q.13: What is the output?

```
class Program {
        static void wrapperOps() {
                Integer inObj = new Integer(10);
                int  i = inObj;
                System.out.println(i);
        }

        public static void main(String args[]) {
```

	wrapperOps();
	        }
	}

A	10.
B	Runtime error.
C	11.
D	Compiler error.
	<----Right Answer

Q.14: What is the output?

```
class Program {
        static void wrapperOps() {
                Integer inObj = new Integer(10);
                short  i = (short) inObj;
                System.out.println(i);
        }

        public static void main(String args[]) {
        wrapperOps();
        }
}
```

A	Compiler error.
B	10.
C	Runtime error.
D	11.
	<----Right Answer

Q.15: Which of the following wrapper classes cannot be assigned 'null' value.

A	Integer.
B	Float.
C	Double.
D	None of the above.
	<----Right Answer

Q.16: Which of the following wrapper classes cannot be added in to a collection.

A	Long.
B	Boolean.
C	Short.

D	None of the above.
	<----Right Answer

Q.17: What is the output?

```
class Program {
        static void wrapperOps() {
                int i=10;
                Integer iw = i;
                System.out.println(iw);
        }

        public static void main(String args[]) {
        wrapperOps();
        }
}
```

A	Compiler error.
B	Runtime error.
C	10.
D	Object.10
	<----Right Answer

Q.18: What is the output?

```
class Program {
        static void wrapperOps() {
                int i=10;
                Integer iw = i;
                int j=iw;
                System.out.println(j);
        }

        public static void main(String args[]) {
        wrapperOps();
        }
}
```

A	10.
B	11.
C	12.
D	Compiler error.
	<----Right Answer

Q.19: What is autoboxing?

A	Converting primitive type to wrapper class.
B	Converting wrapper class to primitive type.
C	Converting primitive to object.
D	Converting object to primitive.
	<----Right Answer

Q.20: What is the output?

```
class Program {
        static void wrapperOps() {
                Integer inObj = new Integer(10);
                long ll = inObj;
                System.out.println(ll);
        }

        public static void main(String args[]) {
        wrapperOps();
        }
}
```

A	10.
B	Compiler error.
C	11.
D	Runtime error.
	<----Right Answer

Q.21: When a primitive is converted to wrapper class it is called as ....

A	Boxing.
B	Autoboxing.
C	Unboxing.
D	Auto unboxing.
	<----Right Answer

Q.22: When a wrapper class is converted to primitive type it is called as ....

A	Boxing.
B	Autoboxing.
C	Unboxing.
D	Auto unboxing.
	<----Right Answer

Answers:

Q.No	Ans	Explanation
1	D	String does not have wrapper class.
2	D	Object does not have wrapper class.
3	B	Wrapper class for boolean type is Boolean class.
4	A	Wrapper class for double type is Double class.
5	C	Wrapper class for char type is Character class.
6	D	Wrapper class for float type is Float class.
7	A	Wrapper class for byte type is Byte class.
8	D	Wrapper class for long type is Long class.
9	B	Wrapper class for int type is Integer class.
10	C	Wrapper class for short type is Short class.
11	B	Converting wrapper class to primitive type is called as unboxing.
12	B	'int' data type cannot be assigned to short wrapper class.
13	A	By computation the result is 10.
14	A	Integer wrapper type cannot be converted to short type.
15	D	All can be assigned 'null' value.
16	D	All can be added to a collection.
17	C	By computation the result is 10.
18	A	By computation the result is 10.
19	A	Converting primitive type to wrapper class is called as autoboxing.
20	A	By computation the result is 10.
21	B	When a primitive is converted to wrapper class it is called as Autoboxing.
22	C	When a wrapper class is converted to primitive type it is called as Unboxing.

Chapter 9
Conditional Constructs

	Q.1: Identify the decision construct in Java.
A	if.
B	switch.
C	find.
D	perform.
	<----Right Answer

	Q.2: Identify the invalid syntax of 'if' condition.
A	if(condition)
B	if(condition) <instructions> else <instructions>
C	if(condition) <instructions> elseif <instructions> else <instructions>
D	elseif(condition) <instructions> elseif <instructions> else <instructions>
	<----Right Answer

Q.3: What is the output?

```
class Program {
 static void ifOps() {
        int i=10;
        if (i > 5)
                System.out.println(i);
 }
 public static void main(String args[]) {
        ifOps();
 }
}
```

A	10
B	5
C	No output.
D	None of the above.
	<----Right Answer

Q.4: What is the output?

```
class Program {
```

```
static void ifOps() {
      int i=10;
      int j=i*5;
      if (i > 15)
              System.out.println(i);
              System.out.println(j);
}
public static void main(String args[]) {
      ifOps();
}
}
```

A	10
	50
B	50
C	5
	50
D	No output.
	<----Right Answer

Q.5: What is the output?

```
class Program {
 static void ifOps() {
      int i=10;
      int j=i*5;
      if (i > 15)
              System.out.println(i);
      else
              System.out.println(j);
}
public static void main(String args[]) {
      ifOps();
}
}
```

A	10
B	50
C	5
D	Compiler error.
	<----Right Answer

Q.6: What is the output?

```
class Program {
 static void ifOps() {
      int i=10;
```

```
        int j=i*5;
        if (i > 15)
            System.out.println(i);
        else
            System.out.println(j);
        else
            System.out.println(i*j);
    }
    public static void main(String args[]) {
        ifOps();
    }
}
```

A	500
B	Compiler error.
C	10
D	50
	<----Right Answer

Q.7: What is the output?

```
class Program {
  static void ifOps() {
        int i=10;
        int j=i*5;
        if (i > 15)
                System.out.println(i);
        else if(j>20)
                System.out.println(j);
        else
            System.out.println(i*j);
    }
    public static void main(String args[]) {
        ifOps();
    }
}
```

A	10
B	500
C	50
D	Compiler error.
	<----Right Answer

Q.8: What is the output?

```
class Program {
  static void ifOps() {
```

```
        int i=10;
        int j=i*5;
        if (i > 5)
                System.out.println(i);
        else if(j>20)
                System.out.println(j);
        else
           System.out.println(i*j);
  }
 public static void main(String args[]) {
        ifOps();
  }
}
```

A	500
B	50
C	10
D	Compiler error.
	<----Right Answer

Q.9: What is the output?

```
class Program {
 static void ifOps() {
        int i=2;
        int j=i*2;
        if (i > 5)
                System.out.println(i);
        else if(j>20)
                System.out.println(j);
        else
           System.out.println(i*j);
  }
 public static void main(String args[]) {
        ifOps();
  }
}
```

A	2
B	4
C	8
D	Compiler error.
	<----Right Answer

Q.10: What is the output?

```
class Program {
```

```
static void ifOps() {
       int i=10;
       int j=i*5;
       if (i > 15)
              System.out.println(j);
              System.out.println(i);
}
public static void main(String args[]) {
       ifOps();
}
}
```

A	50
B	5
C	10
D	50
	10
	<----Right Answer

Q.11: What is the output?

```
class Program {
 static void ifOps() {
       int i=2;
       int j=i*2;
       if (i==2)
              System.out.println(j);
       else if(j==4)
              System.out.println(i);

}
public static void main(String args[]) {
       ifOps();
}
}
```

A	2
B	4
C	8
D	Compiler error.
	<----Right Answer

Q.12: What is the output?

```
class Program {
 static void ifOps() {
       int i=2;
```

```
            int j=i*2;
            if (i=2)
                    System.out.println(i);
            else if(j=4)
                    System.out.println(j);


    }
    public static void main(String args[]) {
            ifOps();
    }
}
```

A	2
B	4
C	8
D	Compiler error.
	<----Right Answer

Q.13: What is the output?

```
class Program {
 static void ifOps() {
            int i=2;
            int j=i*2;
            if (i=j)
                    System.out.println(i);

            System.out.println(j);

    }
    public static void main(String args[]) {
            ifOps();
    }
}
```

A	2
B	4
C	8
D	Compiler error.
	<----Right Answer

Q.14: What is the output?

```
class Program {
 static void ifOps() {
            boolean b;
            if (b)
```

```
                System.out.println(false);
        else
                System.out.println(true);

}
public static void main(String args[]) {
        ifOps();
}
}
```

A	true.
B	false.
C	Compiler error.
D	Runtime error.
	<----Right Answer

Q.15: What is the output?

```
class Program {
 static void ifOps() {
        boolean b=false;
        if (b)
                System.out.println(false);
        else
                System.out.println(true);

}
public static void main(String args[]) {
        ifOps();
}
}
```

A	false.
B	Compiler error.
C	true.
D	Runtime error.
	<----Right Answer

Q.16: What is the output?

```
class Program {
 static void ifOps() {
        boolean b=true;
        if (b==true)
                System.out.println(false);
        else
                System.out.println(true);
```

```
        }
        public static void main(String args[]) {
              ifOps();
        }
}
```

A	false.
B	true.
C	Compiler error.
D	Runtime error.
	<----Right Answer

Q.17: What is the output?

```
class Program {
  static void ifOps() {
        boolean b=false;
        if (b=true)
                System.out.println(false);
        else
                System.out.println(true);

  }
  public static void main(String args[]) {
        ifOps();
  }
}
```

A	Compiler error.
B	Runtime error.
C	false.
D	true.
	<----Right Answer

Q.18: What is the output?

```
class Program {
  static void ifOps() {
        if (true==true)
                System.out.println(false);
        else
                System.out.println(true);

  }
  public static void main(String args[]) {
        ifOps();
```

	}
	}
A	true.
B	false.
C	Compiler error.
D	None of the above.
	<----Right Answer

Q.19: What is the output?

```
class Program {
 static void ifOps() {
        if (true=true)
                System.out.println(false);
        else
                System.out.println(true);


 }
 public static void main(String args[]) {
        ifOps();
 }
}
```

A	true.
B	false.
C	Runtime error.
D	Compiler error.
	<----Right Answer

Q.20: What is the output?

```
class Program {
 static void ifOps() {
        int i=10;
        int j=i*5;
        if (i > 15)
                System.out.println(j);
                System.out.println(i);
        else
                System.out.println("Failure");
 }
 public static void main(String args[]) {
        ifOps();
 }
}
```

A	Failure.

B	50
	10
C	Compiler error.
D	Runtime error.
	<----Right Answer

Q.21: What is the output?

```java
class Program {
 static void ifOps() {
        boolean b;
        if (b=true)
                System.out.println(false);
        else
                System.out.println(true);

 }
 public static void main(String args[]) {
        ifOps();
 }
}
```

A	true.
B	false.
C	Compiler error.
D	Runtime error.
	<----Right Answer

Q.22: What is the output?

```java
class Program {
 static void ifOps() {
        boolean b=true;
        if (b==1)
                System.out.println(false);
        else
                System.out.println(true);

 }
 public static void main(String args[]) {
        ifOps();
 }
}
```

A	true.
B	false.
C	Complier error.

D	Runtime error.
	<----Right Answer

Q.23: A switch statement is followed by .... Option.

A	case.
B	else.
C	default.
D	any.
	<----Right Answer

Q.24: Which of the following type can be used in a switch statement?

A	float.
B	double.
C	boolean.
D	byte.
	<----Right Answer

Q.25: Which of the following type can be used in a switch statement?

A	char.
B	short.
C	float.
D	boolean.
	<----Right Answer

Q.26: Which of the following type cannot be used in switch case statement?

A	byte.
B	char.
C	short.
D	float.
	<----Right Answer

Q.27: Which of the following type can be used in a switch case statement?

A	int.

B	long.
C	float.
D	single.
	<----Right Answer

Q.28: Which of the following type cannot be used in a switch case statement?

A	int.
B	long.
C	short.
D	char.
	<----Right Answer

Q.29: Which of the following type can be used in a switch case statement?

A	int.
B	long.
C	short.
D	char.
	<----Right Answer

Q.30: How to avoid control falling to next case statement in switch case clause?

A	continue statement.
B	break statement.
C	goto statement.
D	exit() function.
	<----Right Answer

Q.31: .... Option is executed when none of cases are executed.

A	break.
B	default.
C	else.
D	continue.
	<----Right Answer

Q.32: What is the output?

```java
class Program {
 public static void switchOps() {
        int day=5;
        switch(day) {
                case 1:
                        System.out.println("Sunday");
                        break;
                case 2:
                        System.out.println("Monday");
                        break;
                case 3:
                        System.out.println("Tuesday");
                        break;
                case 4:
                        System.out.println("Wednesday");
                        break;
                case 5:
                        System.out.println("Thursday");
                        break;
            case 6:
                System.out.println("Friday");
                        break;
            case 7:                         System.out.println("Saturday");
                        break;
          default:
            System.out.println("Invalid day");
          }
 }
 public static void main(String args[]) {
   switchOps();
 }
}
```

A	Invalid day.
B	Wednesday.
C	Thursday.
D	Friday.
	<----Right Answer

Q.33: What is the output?

```java
class Program {
 public static void switchOps() {
        int day=8;
        switch(day) {
```

```java
                case 1:
                        System.out.println("Sunday");
                        break;
                case 2:
                        System.out.println("Monday");
                        break;
                case 3:
                        System.out.println("Tuesday");
                        break;
                case 4:
                        System.out.println("Wednesday");
                        break;
                case 5:
                        System.out.println("Thursday");
                        break;
                case 6:
                        System.out.println("Friday");
                        break;
                case 7:
                        System.out.println("Saturday");
                        break;
                default:
            System.out.println("Invalid day");
            }
    }
 public static void main(String args[]) {
   switchOps();
 }
}
```

A	Saturday.
B	Invalid day.
C	Monday.
D	Tuesday.
	<----Right Answer

Q.34: What is the output?

```java
class Program {
 public static void switchOps() {
        int day=2;
        switch(day) {
                case 1:
                        System.out.println("Sunday");
                        break;
                case 2:
                        System.out.println("Monday");
```

```
                case 3:
                        System.out.println("Tuesday");
                        break;
                case 4:
                        System.out.println("Wednesday");
                        break;
                case 5:
                        System.out.println("Thursday");
                        break;
                case 6:
                        System.out.println("Friday");
                        break;
                case 7:
                        System.out.println("Saturday");
                        break;
                default:
            System.out.println("Invalid day");
        }
    }
    public static void main(String args[]) {
      switchOps();
    }
}
```

A	Tuesday.
B	Monday Tuesday.
C	Wednesday.
D	Invalid day.
	<----Right Answer

Q.35: What is the output?

```
class Program {
  public static void switchOps() {
        double d = 12.1;
        switch(d) {
                case 12.0:
                        System.out.println("Bangaluru");
                        break;
                case 12.1:
                        System.out.println("Mumbai");
                default:
            System.out.println("Invalid Data");
        }
    }
}
  public static void main(String args[]) {
```

	switchOps();
	 }
	 }

A	Bangaluru.
B	Mumbai.
C	Invalid Data.
D	Compiler error.
	<----Right Answer

Q.36: What is the output?

```
class Program {
 public static void switchOps() {
        char d = 'a';
        switch(d) {
        case 'a':
                System.out.println("Bangaluru");
            break;
        case 'b':
                System.out.println("Mumbai");
            break;
        default:
          System.out.println("Invalid data");
        }
 }
 public static void main(String args[]) {
   switchOps();
 }
}
```

A	Bangaluru.
B	Mumbai.
C	Invalid data.
D	Compiler error.
	<----Right Answer

Q.37: What is the output?

```
class Program {
 public static void switchOps() {
        long l = 123;
        switch(l) {
                case 'a':
                        System.out.println("Bangaluru");
                        break;
                case 'b':
```

```
                System.out.println("Mumbai");
                break;
            default:
        System.out.println("Invalid Data");
        }
    }
public static void main(String args[]) {
    switchOps();
    }
}
```

A	Mumbai.
B	Invalid data.
C	Mumbai.
D	Compiler error.
	<----Right Answer

Q.38: What is the output?

```
class Program {
 public static void switchOps() {
        byte b = 12;
        switch(b) {
            case 'a':
                System.out.println("Bangaluru");
                break;
            case 'b':
                System.out.println("Mumbai");
                break;
            default:
        System.out.println("Invalid data");
        }
    }
 public static void main(String args[]) {
    switchOps();
    }
}
```

A	Bangaluru.
B	Mumbai.
C	Invalid data.
D	Compiler error.
	<----Right Answer

Q.39: What is the output?

```
class Program {
```

```
public static void switchOps() {
        boolean b = true;
        switch(b) {
                case true:
                        System.out.println("Bangaluru");
                        break;
                case false:
                        System.out.println("Mumbai");
                        break;
                default:
            System.out.println("Invalid data");
            }
    }
public static void main(String args[]) {
    switchOps();
    }
}
```

A	Compiler error.
B	Bangaluru.
C	Mumbai.
D	Invalid data.
	<----Right Answer

Q.40: What is the output?

```
class Program {
 public static void switchOps() {
        short sh = 36;
        switch(sh) {
        case 34:
                System.out.println("Bangaluru");
                break;
        case 36:
                System.out.println("Mumbai");
                break;
        default:
            System.out.println("Invalid data");
            }
    }
 public static void main(String args[]) {
    switchOps();
    }
}
```

A	Invalid data.
B	Mumbai.

C	Bangaluru.
D	Compiler error.
	<----Right Answer

Q.41: What is the output?

```
class Program {
 public static void switchOps() {
        float fp = 34.34f;
        switch(fp) {
                case 34.34:
                        System.out.println("Bangaluru");
                        break;
                case 36.36:
                        System.out.println("Mumbai");
                        break;
                default:
            System.out.println("Invalid data");
        }
 }
 public static void main(String args[]) {
   switchOps();
 }
}
```

A	34.34
B	36.36
C	Compiler error.
D	Invalid data.
	<----Right Answer

Q.42: What is the output?

```
class Program {
 public static void switchOps() {
        float fp = 34.34f;
        switch(fp) {
                case 34.34:
                        System.out.println("Bangaluru");
                        break;
                case 36.36:
                        System.out.println("Mumbai");
                        break;
                default:
            System.out.println("Invalid data");
        }
```

```
    }
    public static void main(String args[]) {
      switchOps();
    }
}
```

A	Compiler error.
B	Bangaluru.
C	Mumbai.
D	Invalid data.
	<----Right Answer

Q.43: What is the output?

```
class Program {
  public static void switchOps() {
        int i = 34;
        switch(i) {
        case 34:
                    System.out.println("Bangaluru");
              break;
        case 36:
              System.out.println("Mumbai");
              break;
         default:
           System.out.println("Invalid data");
          }
    }
  public static void main(String args[]) {
    switchOps();
  }
}
```

A	Bangaluru.
B	Mumbai.
C	Invalid data.
D	Compiler error.
	<----Right Answer

Q.44: What is the output?

```
class Program {
  public static void switchOps() {
        String str = "Mysuru";
        switch(str) {
                case "Bangaluru":
                    System.out.println("Bangaluru");
```

```
                    break;
            case "Mumbai":
                    System.out.println("Mumbai");
                    break;
            default:
        System.out.println("Invalid data");
            }
    }
public static void main(String args[]) {
    switchOps();
    }
}
```

A	Bangaluru.
B	Invalid data.
C	Mumbai.
D	Compiler error.
	<----Right Answer

Answers:

Q.No	Ans	Explanation
1	A,B	If and switch are decision making constructs in Java.
2	D	It is the invalid syntax.
3	A	By computation the result is 10.
4	B	By computation the result is 50.
5	B	By computation the result is 50.
6	B	'else' is invalid syntax.
7	C	By computation the result is 50.
8	C	By computation the result is 10.
9	C	By computation the result is 8.
10	C	By computation the result is 10.
11	B	By computation the result is 4.
12	D	'if' condition has invalid syntax.
13	D	'if' condition has invalid syntax.
14	C	Variable not initialized.
15	C	By computation the result is true.

16	A	By computation the result is false.
17	C	By computation the result is false.
18	B	By computation the result is false.
19	D	'if' condition has invalid syntax.
20	C	'if' condition has invalid syntax.
21	B	By computation the result is false.
22	C	'if' condition has invalid syntax.
23	A	Switch is followed by case option.
24	D	'byte' can be used in switch..case.
25	A,B	char, short can be used in switch case.
26	D	'float' cannot be used in switch case.
27	A	'int' can be used in switch case.
28	B	'long' cannot be used in switch case statement.
29	A,C, D	'int, short and char' can be used in switch case statement.
30	B	Break keyword exits a case in switch statement hence control does not fall through to next case.
31	B	Default option is executed when none of the cases are executed.
32	C	By computation the result is 'Thursday'
33	B	By computation the result is 'Invalid day'.
34	B	By computation the result is Monday Tuesday
35	D	Double cannot be used in switch.
36	A	By computation the result is "Bangaluru".
37	D	Long cannot be used in switch case.
38	C	By computation the result is 'Invalid data'.
39	A	Boolean cannot be used in switch case.
40	B	By computation the result is "Mumbai"
41	C	Float cannot be used in switch case.
42	A	Float cannot be used in switch case.
43	A	By computation the result is "Bangaluru".
44	B	By computation the result is "Invalid data".

Chapter 10
Loops

Q.1: Which of the following loop will execute at least once?	
A	while.
B	do..while.
C	for.
D	until.
	<----Right Answer

Q.2: How to exit a loop?	
A	break keyword.
B	continue keyword.
C	exit keyword.
D	quit keyword.
	<----Right Answer

Q.3: Identify the correct syntax of 'for' loop.	

A	for (initialization; condition; increment) {
	      instructions;
	   }

B	for (condition;initialization; increment) {
	      instructions;
	   }

C	for (increment;initialization; condition) {
	      instructions;
	   }

D	for (initialization; increment;condition) {
	      instructions;
	   }

	<----Right Answer

Q.4: What is the output?
class Program {   static void forOps() {

```
            int i=0;
            for(i=10; i>0;i--)
                    i--;

            System.out.println(i);
        }
        public static void main(String args[]) {
                forOps();
        }
}
```

A	10
B	1
C	0
D	Compiler error.
	<----Right Answer

Q.5: What is the output?

```
class Program {
        static void forOps() {
                int i=10;
                for(;;)
                        i--;
        }
        public static void main(String args[]) {
                forOps();
        }
}
```

A	Compiler error.
B	0
C	Runtime error.
D	Infinite loop.
	<----Right Answer

Q.6: How to exit an inner loop?

A	continue keyword.
B	goto keyword.
C	break keyword.
D	exit keyword.
	<----Right Answer

Q.7: How to return the control to start of a loop?

A	exit keyword.
B	break keyword.
C	goto keyword.
D	continue keyword.
	<----Right Answer

Q.8: What is the output?

```
class Program {
        static void forOps() {
                for(int i=10; i>0;i--)
                        i--;
                System.out.println(i);
        }
        public static void main(String args[]) {
                forOps();
        }
}
```

A	10
B	0
C	Compiler error.
D	1
	<----Right Answer

Q.9: What is the output?

```
class Program {
        static void forOps() {
                int i=10;
                for(;;)
                        i--;
                System.out.println(i);
        }
        public static void main(String args[]) {
                forOps();
        }
}
```

A	Compiler error.
B	Runtime error.
C	Infinite loop.
D	0
	<----Right Answer

Q.10: What is the output?

```
class Program {
        static void forOps() {
                int i;
                for(i=0;i<2;i++)
                        System.out.println(i);
                        System.out.println(i);
        }
        public static void main(String args[]) {
                forOps();
        }
}
```

A	0
	0
	1
	1
	2
	2
B	0
	1
	2
C	1
	2
	3
D	0
	<----Right Answer

Q.11: What is the output?

```
class Program {
        static void forOps() {
                int i;
                for(i=0;i<2;i++);
                        System.out.println(i);

        }
        public static void main(String args[]) {
                forOps();
        }
}
```

A	Compiler error.
B	1
C	2
D	0
	1

	2
	<----Right Answer

Q.12: What is the output?	

<div>class Program {
    static void forOps() {
        int i;
        for(i=0;i<2;i++,System.out.println(i));
 	
    }
    public static void main(String args[]) {
        forOps();
    }
}</div>	

A	0 1 2
B	1 2
C	2
D	Compiler error.
	<----Right Answer

Q.13: What is the output?	

<div>class Program {
    static void forOps() {
        int i;
        for(i=0;i<2;i++);
         System.out.println(i);
 	
    }
    public static void main(String args[]) {
        forOps();
    }
}</div>	

A	0 1 2
B	1 2
C	2
D	Compiler error.
	<----Right Answer

Q.14: What is the output?

```
class Program {
        static void forOps() {
                int i=0;
                for(double d=4.5,i=1;i<2;i++)
                    System.out.println(i);


        }
        public static void main(String args[]) {
                forOps();
        }
}
```

A	Compiler error.
B	1
C	2
D	1 2
	<----Right Answer

Q.15: What is the output?

```
class Program {
        static void forOps() {
          for(int i=0,double d=4.5;i<2;i++)
                    System.out.println(i);


        }
        public static void main(String args[]) {
                forOps();
        }
}
```

A	1
B	1 2
C	0 1 2
D	Compiler error.
	<----Right Answer

Q.16: What is the output?

```
class Program {
        static void forOps() {
```

```
                    int i;
                    for(i=0;i<3;i++,System.out.println(i));


            }
            public static void main(String args[]) {
                    forOps();
            }
}
```

A	1
	2
	3
B	0
	1
	2
	3
C	3
D	Compiler error.
	<----Right Answer

Q.17: What is the output?

```
class Program {
 static void forOps() {
    int i=0;
 for(int j=10;i<2;i++) System.out.println(i);



 }
 public static void main(String args[]) {
        forOps();
 }
}
```

A	0
B	0
	1
C	0
	1
	2
D	Compiler error.
	<----Right Answer

Q.18: What is the output?

```
class Program {
        static void forOps() {
```

```
                int i,k=0;
                for(i=0;i<1;i++)
                        for(int j=0;j<1;j++)
                                k++;
                            System.out.println(i);
        }
        public static void main(String args[]) {
                forOps();
        }
}
```

A	0
	0
B	0
	0
	1
C	0
	0
	1
	1
D	1
	<----Right Answer

Q.19: What is the output?

```
class Program {
        static void forOps() {
                int i;
                for(i=0;i<6;i++) {
                        if (i>4)
                                break;
                }
                System.out.println(i);
        }
        public static void main(String args[]) {
                forOps();
        }
}
```

A	4
B	5
C	6
D	3
	<----Right Answer

Q.20: What is the output?

```
class Program {
        static void forOps() {
                int i;
                for(i=0;i<6;i++) {
                        if (i>4)
                                continue;
                }
                System.out.println(i);
        }
        public static void main(String args[]) {
                forOps();
        }
}
```

A	5
B	4
C	7
D	6
	<----Right Answer

Q.21: What is the output?

```
class Program {
        static void forOps() {
                int i=0;
                boolean b=true;
                for(i=0;b;i++)
                        b=false;
                System.out.println(i);
        }
        public static void main(String args[]) {
                forOps();
        }
}
```

A	False
B	True
C	0
D	1
	<----Right Answer

Q.22: What is the output?

```
class Program {
 static void whileOps() {
        int i=10;
        while (i > 1)
```

```
        i--;
        System.out.println(i);
   }
 public static void main(String args[]) {
  whileOps();
 }
}
```

A	Compiler error.
B	0
C	1
D	2
	<----Right Answer

Q.23: What is the output?

```
class Program {
 static void whileOps() {
        boolean b=false;
        while (b) {
                b=true;
                System.out.println(b);
        }
 }
 public static void main(String args[]) {
  whileOps();
 }
}
```

A	true.
B	false.
C	Compiler error.
D	No output.
	<----Right Answer

Q.24: What is the output?

```
class Program {
 static void whileOps() {
        boolean b=true;
        while (b) {
                b=false;
                continue;
                System.out.println(b);
        }
 }
 public static void main(String args[]) {
```

	whileOps();
	}
	}
A	true.
B	false.
C	No output.
D	Compiler error.
	<----Right Answer

Q.25: What is the output?

```
class Program {
        static void forOps() {
                int i=0;
                boolean b=false;
                for(i=0;b;i++)
                        b=true;
                System.out.println(i);
        }
        public static void main(String args[]) {
                forOps();
        }
}
```

A	true.
B	1
C	false.
D	0
	<----Right Answer

Q.26: .... Loop's condition is checked after one iteration.

A	for.
B	while.
C	do..while.
D	for in.
	<----Right Answer

Q.27: What is the output?

```
class Program {
 static void whileOps() {
        boolean b=true;
        while (b) {
                b=false;
```

```
            break;
            System.out.println(b);
        }
    }
    public static void main(String args[]) {
      whileOps();
    }
}
```

A	true.
B	false.
C	No output.
D	Compiler error.
	<----Right Answer

Q.28: What is the output?

```
class Program {
  static void whileOps() {
        boolean b=true;
        while (b) {
                b=false;
                if(b)
                    break;
                else
                  System.out.println(b);
        }
    }
    public static void main(String args[]) {
      whileOps();
    }
}
```

A	true.
B	false.
C	No output.
D	Compiler error.
	<----Right Answer

Q.29: What is the output?

```
class Program {
  static void whileOps() {
        boolean b=true;
        while (b) {
                if(b) {
                        b=false;
```

```
                continue;
            }
            else {
                b=true;
                System.out.println(b);
            }
        }
    }
    public static void main(String args[]) {
     whileOps();
    }
}
```

A	true.
B	false.
C	Infinite loop.
D	No output.
	<----Right Answer

Q.30: What is the output?

```
class Program {
 static void dowhileOps() {
   int i=10;
   do {
        i++;
   } while (i<10);
        System.out.println(i);
 }
 public static void main(String args[]) {
   dowhileOps();
 }
}
```

A	10
B	11
C	Compiler error.
D	No output.
	<----Right Answer

Q.31: What is the output?

```
class Program {
 static void dowhileOps() {
   int i=10;
   do
        i++;
```

```
    while (i<10);
        System.out.println(i);
 }
 public static void main(String args[]) {
   dowhileOps();
 }
}
```

A	11
B	10
C	No output.
D	Compiler error.
	<----Right Answer

Q.32: What is the output?

```
class Program {
 static void dowhileOps() {
   int i=10;
   do {
        i++;
        i++;
   }while (i<10);
        System.out.println(i);
 }
 public static void main(String args[]) {
   dowhileOps();
 }
}
```

A	11
B	12
C	10
D	Compiler error.
	<----Right Answer

Q.33: What is the output?

```
class Program {
 static void dowhileOps() {
   int i=10;
   do
        i++;
        i++;
   while (i<10);
        System.out.println(i);
 }
```

```
public static void main(String args[]) {
    dowhileOps();
  }
}
}
```

A	11
B	12
C	10
D	Compiler error.
	<----Right Answer

Q.34: Which loop is specifically used for iterating over aggregates (arrays and collection)?

A	for.
B	while.
C	do while.
D	for each.
	<----Right Answer

Q.35: For each loop was introduced in version .... of Java.

A	7
B	6
C	5
D	8
	<----Right Answer

Q.36: Which of the following does not have a condition check?

A	for each.
B	for.
C	while.
D	do while.
	<----Right Answer

Q.37: What is the output?

```
class Program {
        static void foreachOps() {
                int ar[] = {6,7};
                for(int i : ar)
                    System.out.print(i);
```

```
        }

        public static void main(String args[]) {
                foreachOps();
        }
}
```

A	6
B	7
C	67
D	76
	<----Right Answer

Q.38: What is the output?

```
class Program {
        static void foreachOps() {
                int ar[] = {6,7};
                for(int i : ar) {
                        break;
                    System.out.print(i);
                }
        }
        public static void main(String args[]) {
                foreachOps();
        }
}
```

A	6
B	7
C	Compiler error.
D	No output.
	<----Right Answer

Q.39: Identify the syntax.

```
for(data_type variable : array | collection)  { }
```

A	For loop.
B	For each loop.
C	Jag array.
D	None of the above.
	<----Right Answer

Q.40: Identify the error in code.	

1.class Program {
2.   static void foreachOps() {
3.   int ar[][] = {{13,22},{36,43}};
4.   for(int i[] : ar)
5.   for (int j : i)
6.   System.out.print(j+" ");
7.   }
8.   public static void main(String args[]) {
9.   foreachOps();
10.   }
11. }	

A	Line 3.
B	Line 4.
C	Line 5.
D	No error.
	<----Right Answer

Answers:

Q.No	Ans	Explanation
1	B	Do.. while loop executes at least once.
2	A	'break' keyword is used for exiting a loop.
3	A	Correct syntax.
4	C	By computation the result is 0.
5	D	It is an infinite loop.
6	C	'break' is used for exiting a loop.
7	D	'continue' keyword is used for returning the control to start of a loop.
8	C	Code not reachable.
9	A	Code not reachable.
10	B	By computation the result is 0 1 2
11	C	By computation the result is 2.
12	B	By computation the result is 1

131

		2
13	C	By computation the result is 2.
14	A	Invalid code.
15	D	Invalid code.
16	A	By computation the result is 1 2
17	B	By computation the result is 0 1
18	D	By computation the result is 1.
19	B	By computation the result is 5.
20	D	By computation the result is 6.
21	D	By computation the result is 1.
22	C	By computation the result is 1.
23	D	No output.
24	D	Unreachable code.
25	D	By computation the result is 0.
26	C	Do.. while loop condition is checked after one iteration.
27	D	Unreachable code.
28	B	By computation the result is false.
29	D	No output.
30	B	By computation the result is 11.
31	A	By computation the result is 11.
32	B	By computation the result is 12.
33	D	Invalid code
34	D	For each loop is used for iterating over arrays and collections.
35	C	For each was added to java in version 5.
36	A	For each loop does not have condition check.
37	C	By computation the result is 67.
38	C	Code not reachable.
39	B	Syntax is of for each loop.
40	D	There is no error in the code.

Chapter 11
Operators

Q.1: Which operator works with 1 operand?	
A	+
B	-
C	*
D	++
	<----Right Answer

Q.2: Which operator works with 2 operands?	
A	++
B	--
C	%
D	!
	<----Right Answer

Q.3: Which operator works with 3 operands?	
A	*
B	++
C	%
D	None of the above
	<----Right Answer

Q.4: Identify the modulus operator.	
A	^
B	#
C	&&
D	%
	<----Right Answer

Q.5: Identify the logical OR operator.	
A	&&

B	!
C	||
D	|
	<----Right Answer

Q.6: Identify the bitwise AND operator.

A	|
B	!
C	&
D	%
	<----Right Answer

Q.7: Identify the logical NOT operator.

A	!
B	&
C	&&
D	||
	<----Right Answer

Q.8: Identify the logical AND operator.

A	||
B	&&
C	%
D	!
	<----Right Answer

Q.9: Which operator works with 4 operands?

A	||
B	^
C	!
D	None of the above.
	<----Right Answer

Q.10: Identify the ternary operator.

A	^
B	?
C	#
D	()
	<----Right Answer

Q.11: What is the output?

```
class Program {
        static void myFx() {
                int i=10,j=0;
                int k = i%j;
                System.out.println(k);
        }
        public static void main(String args[]) {
                myFx();
        }
}
```

A	0
B	10
C	Runtime error.
D	Compiler error.
	<----Right Answer

Q.12: What is the output?

```
class Program {
        static void myFx() {
                int i=10,j=10;
                if(i===j)
                  System.out.println("Equals");
        }
        public static void main(String args[]) {
                myFx();
        }
}
```

A	Equals.
B	No output.
C	Compiler error.
D	Runtime error.
	<----Right Answer

Q.13: What is the output?

```
class Program {
```

```
static void myFx() {
        int i=10,j=10;
         System.out.println(i==j);
}
public static void main(String args[]) {
        myFx();
}
}
```

A	false.
B	true.
C	10
D	Compiler error.
	<----Right Answer

Q.14: What is the output?

```
class Program {
        static void myFx() {
                int i=10,j=11;
                 System.out.println(i!=j);
        }
        public static void main(String args[]) {
                myFx();
        }
}
```

A	10
B	Compiler error.
C	true.
D	false.
	<----Right Answer

Q.15: What is the output?

```
class Program {
        static void myFx() {
                int i=10,j=11;
                System.out.println(i<>j);
        }
        public static void main(String args[]) {
                myFx();
        }
}
```

A	true.
B	false.
C	10

D	Compiler error.
	<----Right Answer

Q.16: What is the output?

```
class Program {
        static void myFx() {
                int i=10,j=11;

        if(i>9 || j<10)
          System. out.println("Success");
        else
          System.out.println("Failure");


        }
        public static void main(String args[]) {
                myFx();
        }
}
```

A	Success.
B	Failure.
C	Compiler error.
D	Runtime error.
	<----Right Answer

Q.17: Identify the XOR operator.

A	&&
B	||
C	!
D	^
	<----Right Answer

Q.18: What is the output?

```
class Program {
        static void myFx() {
                int i=10,j=11;

        if (i>9 && j < 10)
        System.out.println("Success");
        else                    System.out.println("Failure");
        }
        public static void main(String args[]) {
```

	myFx();
	}
}	
A	Success.
B	Failure.
C	Compiler error.
D	No output.
	<----Right Answer

Q.19: What is the output?

```
class Program {
        static void myFx() {
        int i=10,j=11;

        if (i>9 ^ j < 10)
                System.out.println("Success");
        else
                System.out.println("Failure");
        }
        public static void main(String args[]) {
                myFx();
        }
}
```

A	Success.
B	Failure.
C	No output.
D	Compiler error.
	<----Right Answer

Q.20: What is the output?

```
class Program {
        static void myFx() {
                int i=11,j=11;

                if (i>9 ^ j < 12)
                        System.out.println("Success");
                else
                        System.out.println("Failure");

        }
        public static void main(String args[]) {
                myFx();
        }
```

	}
A	Failure.
B	Success.
C	No output.
D	Compiler error.
	<----Right Answer

Q.21: What is the output?

```
class Program {
        static void myFx() {
                int i=11,j=13;

                if (i>9 ^ j < 12)
                        System.out.println("Success");
                else
                        System.out.println("Failure");

        }
        public static void main(String args[]) {
                myFx();
        }
}
```

A	Failure.
B	Success.
C	No output.
D	Compiler error.
	<----Right Answer

Q.22: What is the output?

```
class Program {
        static void myFx() {
                int i=11;

                if ( ! (i>9) )
                        System.out.println("Success");
                else
                        System.out.println("Failure");
        }
        public static void main(String args[]) {
                myFx();
        }
}
```

A	Failure.

B	Success.
C	Compiler error.
D	No output.
	<----Right Answer

Q.23: What is the output?

```
class Program {
        static void myFx() {
                int i=18;

                if ( ! (i<9) )
                        System.out.println("Success");
                else
                        System.out.println("Failure");
        }
        public static void main(String args[]) {
                myFx();
        }
}
```

A	Failure.
B	Success.
C	Compiler error.
D	No output.
	<----Right Answer

Q.24: What is the output?

```
class Program {
        static void myFx() {
                int i=11,j=11;

                if (i<9 || j >12)
                        System.out.println("Success");
                else
                        System.out.println("Failure");
        }
        public static void main(String args[]) {
                myFx();
        }
}
```

A	Failure.
B	Success.
C	Compiler error.
D	No output.

Q.25: What is the output?

```
class Program {
 static void instOps() {
        Program obj = new Program();
        if (obj instanceof Program)
                System.out.println("Success");
        else
                System.out.println("Failure");
 }
 public static void main(String args[]) {
    instOps();
 }
}
```

A	Success.
B	Failure.
C	No output.
D	Compiler error.
	<----**Right Answer**

Q.26: What is the output?

```
class Program {
 static void instOps() {
        Program obj = null;
        if (obj instanceof Program)
                System.out.println("Success");
        else
                System.out.println("Failure");
 }
 public static void main(String args[]) {
    instOps();
 }
}
```

A	Success.
B	Failure.
C	No output.
D	Compiler error.
	<----**Right Answer**

Q.27: What is the output?
class Program {

```
static void myFx() {
    int i=11,j=11;

    if (i<9 && j >12)
        System.out.println("Success");
    else
        System.out.println("Failure");
}
public static void main(String args[]) {
    myFx();
}
}
```

A	Failure.
B	Success.
C	Compiler error.
D	No output.
	<----Right Answer

Q.28: What is the output?

```
class Program {
    static void myFx() {
        int i=11,j=11;

        if ( ! i>9 )
            System.out.println("Success");
        else
            System.out.println("Failure");
    }
    public static void main(String args[]) {
        myFx();
    }
}
```

A	Failure
B	Success.
C	Compiler error.
D	No output.
	<----Right Answer

Q.29: What is the output?

```
class Program {
    static void myFx() {
        int i=11,j=11;
```

```
        if ( i<9 && j< 10)
            System.out.println("Success");
        else
                System.out.println("Failure");
        }
        public static void main(String args[]) {
                myFx();
        }
}
```

A	Failure.
B	Success.
C	Compiler error.
D	No output.
	<----Right Answer

Q.30: What is the output?

```
class Program {
 static void instOps() {
        int i=10;
        if (i instanceof int)
                System.out.println("Success");
        else
                System.out.println("Failure");
}
 public static void main(String args[]) {
   instOps();
 }
}
```

A	Success.
B	Failure.
C	Runtime error.
D	Compiler error.
	<----Right Answer

Q.31: What is the output?

```
class Program {
  static void terOps() {
        int j=10;
        String result = j<10 ? "Failure" : "Success";
        System.out.println(result);
  }

  public static void main(String args[]) {
```

```
        terOps();
  }
}
```

A	Success.
B	Failure.
C	No output.
D	Compiler error.
	<----Right Answer

Q.32: What is the output?

```
class Program {
 static void instOps() {
        boolean b=true;
        if (b instanceof boolean)
                System.out.println("Success");
        else
                System.out.println("Failure");
 }
 public static void main(String args[]) {
   instOps();
 }
}
```

A	Success.
B	Failure.
C	No output.
D	Compiler error.
	<----Right Answer

Q.33: What is the output?

```
class Program {
 static void instOps() {
        String str="Java";
        if (str instanceof String)
                System.out.println("Success");
        else
                System.out.println("Failure");
 }
 public static void main(String args[]) {
   instOps();
 }
}
```

| A | Success. |
| B | No output. |

C	Compiler error.
D	Failure.
	<----Right Answer

Q.34: What is the output?

```
class Program {
  static void terOps() {
      int j=10;
      String result = false ? "Failure" : "Success";
      System.out.println(result);
  }

  public static void main(String args[]) {
      terOps();
  }
}
```

A	Success.
B	Failure.
C	No output.
D	Compiler error.
	<----Right Answer

Q.35: What is the output?

```
class Program {
  static void terOps() {
      int j=10,i=11;
      String result = (j>10 ^ i < 12)? "Failure" : "Success";
      System.out.println(result);
  }

  public static void main(String args[]) {
      terOps();
  }
}
```

A	Success.
B	Failure.
C	Compiler error.
D	No output.
	<----Right Answer

Q.36: What is the output?
class Program {

```
    static void terOps() {
        int j=10,i=11;
        String result = !(j>10 ^ i < 12)? "Failure" : "Success";
        System.out.println(result);
    }

  public static void main(String args[]) {
        terOps();
    }
}
```

A	Success.
B	Failure.
C	No output.
D	Compiler error.
	<----Right Answer

Q.37: What is the output?

```
class Program {
  static void terOps() {
        int j=10,i=11;
        String result = !(j>10 && i < 12)? "Failure" : "Success";
        System.out.println(result);
    }

  public static void main(String args[]) {
        terOps();
    }
}
```

A	Success.
B	Failure.
C	Compiler error.
D	No output.
	<----Right Answer

Q.38: What is the output?

```
class Program {
  static void terOps() {
        int j=10,i=11,k=25;
        String result = !(j>10 && i < 12 && k > 10)? "Failure" : "Success";
        System.out.println(result);
    }

  public static void main(String args[]) {
```

146

	terOps();
	}
	}
A	Success.
B	Failure.
C	Compiler error.
D	Runtime error.
	<----Right Answer

Q.39: What is the output?

```
class Program {
  static void terOps() {
      int j=10;
      String result = !(j==10)? "Failure" : "Success";
      System.out.println(result);
  }

  public static void main(String args[]) {
      terOps();
  }
}
```

A	Success.
B	Failure.
C	No output.
D	Compiler error.
	<----Right Answer

Q.40: What is the output?

```
class Program {
  static void terOps() {
      int j=10;
      String result = true ? "Failure" : "Success";
      System.out.println(result);
  }

  public static void main(String args[]) {
      terOps();
  }
}
```

A	Compiler error.
B	Success.
C	Failure.
D	No output.

<----Right Answer

Q.41: What is the output?

```
class Program {
 static void instOps() {
        Object obj="Java";
        if (obj instanceof Object)
                System.out.println("Success");
        else
                System.out.println("Failure");
 }
 public static void main(String args[]) {
    instOps();
 }
}
```

A	Success.
B	Failure.
C	No output.
D	Compiler error.
	<----Right Answer

Q.42: What is the output?

```
class Program {
 static void instOps() {
        Object obj="Java";
        String str = !(obj instanceof Object) ? "Success" : "Failure";

        System.out.println(str);
 }
 public static void main(String args[]) {
    instOps();
 }
}
```

A	Success.
B	Failure.
C	No output.
D	Compiler error.
	<----Right Answer

Answers:

Q.No	Ans	Explanation
1	D	'++' is a unary operator.
2	C	'%' is a binary operator.
3	D	There is no operator that works with 3 operands.
4	D	'%' is the modulus operator.
5	C	'||' is the logical OR operator.
6	C	'&' is the bitwise AND operator.
7	A	'!' is the NOT operator.
8	B	'&&' is the logical AND operator.
9	D	There is no operator that works with 4 operands.
10	B	'?' is the ternary operator.
11	C	Division by yields a exception.
12	C	The expression is invalid.
13	B	By computation the result is 'true'.
14	C	By computation the result is 'true'.
15	D	The expression is invalid.
16	A	By computation the result is 'Success'.
17	D	'^' is the XOR operator.
18	B	By computation the result is 'Failure'.
19	A	By computation the result is 'Success'.
20	A	By computation the result is 'Failure'.
21	B	By computation the result is 'Success'.
22	A	By computation the result is 'Failure'.
23	B	By computation the result is 'Success'.
24	A	By computation the result is 'Failure'.
25	A	By computation the result is 'Success'.
26	B	By computation the result is 'Success'.
27	A	By computation the result is 'Failure'.
28	C	The expression is invalid.
29	A	By computation the result is 'Failure'.
30	D	The expression is invalid.
31	A	By computation the result is 'Success'.

32	D	The expression is invalid.
33	A	By computation the result is 'Success'.
34	A	By computation the result is 'Success'.
35	B	By computation the result is 'Failure'.
36	A	By computation the result is 'Success'.
37	B	By computation the result is 'Failure'.
38	B	By computation the result is 'Failure'.
39	A	By computation the result is 'Success'.
40	C	By computation the result is 'Failure'.
41	A	By computation the result is 'Success'.
42	B	By computation the result is 'Failure'.

Chapter 12
Arrays

Q.1: Identify the correct statement.	
A	Array can be of heterogonous type.
B	Array is of a single type.
C	Array size is variable.
D	Java does not support multi dimension arrays.
	<----Right Answer

Q.2: Identify the correct statement.	
A	Java has support for safe arrays.
B	Java does not support safe array.
C	Array are not bounds checked.
D	Array is accessed using a key.
	<----Right Answer

Q.3: Identify the incorrect statement.	
A	Array is accessed using an index.
B	The size of array is fixed.
C	The size of array is variable.
D	Java has support for Multi dimension array.
	<----Right Answer

Q.4: How to get the length of an array.	
A	getSize().
B	getLength().
C	length.
D	sizeof().
	<----Right Answer

Q.5: The index(array) starts at .... location	

A	1
B	User defined.
C	0
D	2
	<----Right Answer

Q.6: .... loop is specifically used for arrays.

A	For.
B	Do while.
C	While.
D	For each.
	<----Right Answer

Q.7: Array is stored on .... Memory by JVM.

A	Stack.
B	Heap.
C	Far.
D	Extended.
	<----Right Answer

Q.8: .... Exception is raised when the array is accessed beyond the bounds.

A	ArrayIndexOutOfBoundsException.
B	ArrayOutOfBoundsException.
C	ArrayBoundsException.
D	ArrayException.
	<----Right Answer

Q.9: Java has support for .... types of array.

A	Single dimension.
B	Two dimension.
C	Three dimension.
D	All of the above.
	<----Right Answer

Q.10: Identify the incorrect syntax.	
A	int [] ar = new int [10];
B	int ar[] = new int[10];
C	int ar[10];
D	int ar[]= new int(10);
	<----Right Answer

Q.11: What is the output?	

```
class Program {
 static void instOps() {
        int []ar = {10,20,30,40};
        int sum=0;
        for (int i=1;i<ar.length-1;i++)
           sum = sum + ar[i];
    System.out.println(sum);
 }
 public static void main(String args[]) {
    instOps();
 }
}
```

A	10
B	30
C	50
D	60
	<----Right Answer

Q.12: What is the output?	

```
class Program {
 static void instOps() {
        int []ar = {10,20,30,40};
        int sum=0;
        for (int i=1;i<ar.length+1;i++)
           sum = sum + ar[i];
    System.out.println(sum);
 }
 public static void main(String args[]) {
    instOps();
 }
}
```

A	100
B	110
C	Compiler error.

D	Runtime error.
	<----Right Answer

Q.13: What is the output?

```
class Program {
 static void instOps() {
        int []ar = {10,20,30,40};
        int sum=0;
        for (int i=0;i<ar.length;i++)
          sum = sum + ar[i];
    System.out.println(sum);
 }
 public static void main(String args[]) {
   instOps();
 }
}
```

A	Compiler error.
B	60
C	50
D	100
	<----Right Answer

Q.14: What is the output?

```
class Program {
 static void instOps() {
        int [][]ar = {{10,20},{30,40},{50,60}};
        int sum=0;

        for (int i=0;i<ar.length;i++)
         for(int j=1;j<ar[0].length+1;j++)
              sum = sum + ar[i][j];

    System.out.println(sum);
 }
 public static void main(String args[]) {
   instOps();
 }
}
```

A	220
B	210
C	Compiler error.
D	Runtime error.
	<----Right Answer

Q.15: What is the output?

```
class Program {
 static void instOps() {
        int [][]ar = {{10,20},{30,40},{50,60}};
        int sum=0;

        for (int i=1;i<ar.length+1;i++)
               for(int j=0;j<ar[0].length;j++)
                      sum = sum + ar[i][j];

    System.out.println(sum);
 }
 public static void main(String args[]) {
   instOps();
 }
}
```

A	190
B	200
C	Compiler error.
D	Runtime error.
	<----Right Answer

Q.16: What is the output?

```
class Program {
 static void instOps() {
        int [][]ar = {{10,20},{30,40},{50,60}};
        int sum=0;

        for (int i=1;i<ar.length;i++)
               for(int j=0;j<ar[0].length;j++)
                      sum = sum + ar[i][j];

    System.out.println(sum);
 }
 public static void main(String args[]) {
   instOps();
 }
}
```

A	180
B	190
C	200
D	Runtime error.
	<----Right Answer

Q.17: What is the output?

```
class Program {
 static void instOps() {
        int [][]ar = {{10,20},{30,40},{50,60}};
        int sum=0;

        for (int i=0;i<ar.length;i++)
                for(int j=0;j<ar[0].length;j++)
                        sum = sum + ar[i][j];

    System.out.println(sum);
 }
 public static void main(String args[]) {
    instOps();
 }
}
```

A	200
B	210
C	220
D	Runtime error.
	<----Right Answer

Q.18: What is the output?

```
class Program {
 static void instOps() {
        int [][]ar = {{10,20},{30,40},{50,60}};
        int sum=0;

        for (int i=1;i<ar.length;i++)
                for(int j=1;j<ar[0].length;j++)
                        sum = sum + ar[i][j];

    System.out.println(sum);
 }
 public static void main(String args[]) {
    instOps();
 }
}
```

A	90
B	100
C	110
D	Compiler error.
	<----Right Answer

Q.19: What is the output?

```
class Program {
 static void instOps() {
        int [][]ar = {{10,20},{30,40},{50,60}};

    System.out.println(ar.length);
 }
 public static void main(String args[]) {
    instOps();
 }
}
```

A	4
B	6
C	5
D	3
	<----Right Answer

Q.20: What is the output?

```
class Program {
 static void instOps() {
        int [][]ar = {{10,20},{30,40},{50,60}};
    System.out.println(ar[2].length);
 }
 public static void main(String args[]) {
    instOps();
 }
}
```

A	2
B	3
C	1
D	Runtime error
	<----Right Answer

Q.21: What is the output?

```
class Program {
 static void instOps() {
    int [][]ar = {{10,20},{30,40},{50,60}};
    System.out.println(ar[0].length);
 }
 public static void main(String args[]) {
    instOps();
 }
}
```

}	
A	3
B	2
C	1
D	Runtime error.
	<----Right Answer

Q.22: Identify Jagged array declaration.

A	int ar[][] = new int[2][2];
B	int ar[][] = new int[2][];
C	int ar[2][] = new int[][];
D	int ar[2][2] = new int[][];
	<----Right Answer

Q.23: Identify the correct syntax.

A	int[][] ar;
B	int [][]ar;
C	int ar()();
D	Int ()()ar;
	<----Right Answer

Q.24: Identify the correct syntax.

A	int ar[][];
B	[]int[] ar;
C	[][]int ar;
D	int []ar[];
	<----Right Answer

Q.25: What is the output?

```
class Program {
 static void instOps() {
        int ar[][][] = new int [2][2][2];
        ar[0][0][0]=5;
        ar[0][0][1]=1;
        ar[0][1][0]=3;
        ar[0][1][1]=8;
        ar[1][0][0]=2;
        ar[1][0][1]=9;
```

```
        ar[1][1][0]=6;
        ar[1][1][1]=4;

    System.out.println(ar[0][1].length);
  }
  public static void main(String args[]) {
    instOps();
  }
}
```

A	1
B	2
C	3
D	Runtime error.
	<----Right Answer

Q.26: What is the output?

```
class Program {
  static void instOps() {
        int [][]ar = {{10,20},{30,40},{50,60}};
    System.out.println(ar[3].length);
  }
  public static void main(String args[]) {
    instOps();
  }
}
```

A	2
B	1
C	3
D	Runtime error.
	<----Right Answer

Q.27: What is the output?

```
class Program {
  static void instOps() {
        int ar[][][] = new int [2][3][3];
        ar[0][0][0]=5;
        ar[0][0][1]=1;
        ar[0][1][0]=3;
        ar[0][1][1]=8;
        ar[1][0][0]=2;
        ar[1][0][1]=9;
        ar[1][1][0]=6;
        ar[1][1][1]=4;
```

```
    System.out.println(ar[1].length);
  }
 public static void main(String args[]) {
    instOps();
  }
}
```

A	1
B	2
C	3
D	Runtime error.
	<----Right Answer

Q.28: What is the output?

```
class Program {
 static void instOps() {
        int ar[][] = new int[3][];
                ar[0]=  new int [1];
                ar[1] = new int[2];
                ar[2] = new int [3];

    System.out.println(ar[1].length);
  }
 public static void main(String args[]) {
    instOps();
  }
}
```

A	2
B	3
C	4
D	Compiler error.
	<----Right Answer

Q.29: What is the output?

```
class Program {
 static void instOps() {
        int ar[][] = new int[3][];
                ar[0]=  new int [1];
                ar[1] = new int[2];
                ar[2] = new int [3];

    System.out.println(ar[2].length);
  }
```

```
    public static void main(String args[]) {
        instOps();
    }
}
```

A	3
B	2
C	4
D	Runtime error.
	<----Right Answer

Q.30: What is the output?

```
class Program {
 static void instOps() {
                int ar[][] = new int[3][];
                ar[0]=  new int [1];
                ar[1] = new int[2];
                ar[2] = new int [3];

    System.out.println(ar[3].length);
 }
 public static void main(String args[]) {
    instOps();
 }
}
```

A	2
B	3
C	4
D	Runtime error.
	<----Right Answer

Q.31: What is the output?

```
class Program {
        static void jaggOps() {
                int ar[][] = new int[3][];
                int sum=0;

                ar[0] = new int [1];
                ar[1] = new int[2];
                ar[2] = new int [3];
        for(int i=0;i<ar.length;i++)
                for(int j=0;j<ar[i].length;j++)
                                ar[i][j] = i*j;
```

```
        for(int i=0;i<ar.length;i++)
          for(int j=0;j<ar[i].length;j++)
                    sum = ar[i][j] + sum;

        System.out.println(sum);
        }
        public static void main(String args[]) {
              jaggOps();
        }


}
```

A	5
B	6
C	7
D	8
	<----Right Answer

Q.32: What is the output?

```
class Program {
      static void myFx() {
            int ar[][] = {{2,3},{4,5},{6,8}};
                  int sum=0;

            for (int []i : ar)
                  for (int j : i)
                        sum = sum + j;

            System.out.println(sum);
      }
      public static void main(String args[]) {
            myFx();
      }


}
```

A	26
B	27
C	25
D	28
	<----Right Answer

Q.33: What is the output?

```
class Program {
      static void myFx() {
```

```
            int sum=0;
            int ar[][] = new int[3][];
            ar[0] = new int [1];
            ar[1] = new int[2];
            ar[2] = new int [3];
            for(int i=0;i<ar.length;i++)
             for(int j=0;j<ar[i].length;j++)
                         ar[i][j] = i*j;

            for (int []i : ar)
                    for (int j : i)
                            sum = sum + j;

            System.out.println(sum);
      }
      public static void main(String args[]) {
            myFx();
      }
}
```

A	10
B	8
C	7
D	6
	<----Right Answer

Answers:

Q.No	Ans	Explanation
1	B	Array can be of only one data type.
2	A	Array in java are bounds checked hence they are safe.
3	C	The size of array is fixed.
4	C	The length of an array is retrieved by using length property.
5	C	Array index starts at 0.
6	D	For each loop is designed to be used with arrays and collections.
7	B	Array is stored in heap memory.
8	A	ArrayIndexOutOfBoundsException exception is raised when bounds of an array are violated.
9	D	Java has support for following types of arrays

| | | a. 1D |
| | | b. 2D |
		c. Multi dimension
10	C,D	It is the invalid syntax.
11	C	By computation the result is 50.
12	D	Array is bounds checked
13	D	By computation the result is 100.
14	D	Array is bounds checked.
15	D	Array is bounds checked.
16	A	By computation the result is 180.
17	A	By computation the result is 200.
18	C	By computation the result is 110.
19	D	By computation the result is 3.
20	A	By computation the result is 2.
21	B	By computation the result is 2.
22	B	The valid syntax is int ar[][] = new int[2][];
23	A,B	Options are valid syntax.
24	A,D	The expressions are valid.
25	B	By computation the result is 2.
26	D	Invalid access of array.
27	C	By computation the result is 3.
28	A	By computation the result is 2.
29	A	By computation the result is 3.
30	D	Invalid access beyond the bounds.
31	C	By computation the result is 7.
32	D	By computation the result is 28.
33	C	By computation the result is 7.

Chapter 13
Type Casting and Conversion

Q.1: Type conversion occurs between .... types.	
A	Same.
B	Different.
C	Compatible.
D	Integer.
	<----Right Answer

Q.2: Type casting occurs between .... types.	
A	Same.
B	Different.
C	Compatible.
D	Integer.
	<----Right Answer

Q.3: What is the output?

```
class Program {
        static void myFx() {
                byte b=10;
                int i=b;
                System.out.println(i);
        }
        public static void main(String args[]) {
                myFx();
        }
}
```

A	Compiler error.
B	Runtime error.
C	10
D	12
	<----Right Answer

Q.4: What is the output?

```
class Program {
        static void myFx() {
                byte b=10;
                float f=b;
                System.out.println(f);
        }
        public static void main(String args[]) {
                myFx();
        }
}
```

A	Runtime error.
B	10.0
C	Compiler error.
D	12.0
	<----Right Answer

Q.5: What is the output?

```
class Program {
        static void myFx() {
                byte b=10;
                double d=b;
                System.out.println(d);
        }
        public static void main(String args[]) {
                myFx();
        }
}
```

A	10.0
B	12.0
C	Compiler error.
D	Runtime error.
	<----Right Answer

Q.6: What is the output?

```
class Program {
        static void myFx() {
                double d=10.0;
                float f=d;
                System.out.println(f);
        }
        public static void main(String args[]) {
                myFx();
```

	`}`
`}`	
A	10.0
B	12.0
C	Compiler error.
D	Runtime error.
	<----Right Answer

Q.7: What is the output?	
<pre>class Program {
static void myFx() {
float f=10.0f;
double d=f;
System.out.println(d);
}
public static void main(String args[]) {
myFx();
}
}</pre>	
A	12.0
B	10.0
C	Compiler error.
D	Runtime error.
	<----Right Answer

Q.8: What is the output?	
<pre>class Program {
static void myFx() {
double d=10.0;
long l=d;
System.out.println(b);
}
public static void main(String args[]) {
myFx();
}
}</pre>	
A	Runtime error.
B	12.0
C	Compiler error.
D	10.0
	<----Right Answer

Q.9: What is the output?

```
class Program {
        static void myFx() {
                double d=10.0;
                short sh=d;
                System.out.println(b);
        }
        public static void main(String args[]) {
                myFx();
        }
}
```

A	Runtime error.
B	Compiler error.
C	10.0
D	12.0
	<----Right Answer

Q.10: What is the output?

```
class Program {
        static void myFx() {
                float f=10.0f;
                long l=f;
                System.out.println(f);
        }
        public static void main(String args[]) {
                myFx();
        }
}
```

A	10.0
B	12.0
C	Compiler error.
D	Runtime error.
	<----Right Answer

Q.11: What is the output?

```
class Program {
        static void myFx() {
                float f=34.0f;
                short sh=d;
                System.out.println(f);
        }
        public static void main(String args[]) {
                myFx();
```

	}
	}
A	34
B	35
C	Compiler error.
D	Runtime error.
	<----Right Answer

Q.12: What is the output?

```
class Program {
        static void myFx() {
                long l=234;
                float f=l;
                System.out.println(f);
        }
        public static void main(String args[]) {
                myFx();
        }
}
```

A	Compiler error.
B	Runtime error.
C	235.0
D	234.0
	<----Right Answer

Q.13: What is the output?

```
class Program {
        static void myFx() {
                long l=234;
                int i=l;
                System.out.println(i);
        }
        public static void main(String args[]) {
                myFx();
        }
}
```

A	234.0
B	236.0
C	Runtime error.
D	Compiler error.
	<----Right Answer

Q.14: What is the output?	

class Program {
    static void myFx() {
        long l=24;
        double d=l;
        System.out.println(d);
    }
    public static void main(String args[]) {
        myFx();
    }
}	

A	24.0
B	25.0
C	Compiler error.
D	26.0
	<----Right Answer

Q.15: What is the output?	

class Program {
    static void myFx() {
        long l=24;
        short sh=l;
        System.out.println(sh);
    }
    public static void main(String args[]) {
        myFx();
    }
}	

A	24
B	42
C	Compiler error.
D	Runtime error.
	<----Right Answer

Q.16: What is the output?	

class Program {
    static void myFx() {
        boolean b=false;
        byte by=b;
        System.out.println(by);
    }
    public static void main(String args[]) {
        myFx();	

	}
}	
A	Compiler error.
B	Runtime error.
C	1
D	0
	<----Right Answer

Q.17: What is the output?	

class Program {
    static void myFx() {
        int i=99;
        byte b=(byte) i;
        System.out.println(b);
    }
    public static void main(String args[]) {
        myFx();
    }
}	

A	99
B	Compiler error.
C	100
D	Runtime error.
	<----Right Answer

Q.18: What is the output?	

class Program {
    static void myFx() {
        int i=130;
        byte b=(byte) i;
        System.out.println(b);
    }
    public static void main(String args[]) {
        myFx();
    }
}	

A	130
B	Compiler error.
C	-126
D	-127
	<----Right Answer

Q.19: What is the output?	

class Program {
      static void myFx() {
            double d=122.8;
            byte b=(byte) d;
            System.out.println(b);
      }
      public static void main(String args[]) {
            myFx();
      }
}	

A	122
B	123
C	Compiler error.
D	Runtime error.
	<----Right Answer

Q.20: What is the output?	

class Program {
      static void myFx() {
            double d=122.8;
            float f=(float) d;
            System.out.println(f);
      }
      public static void main(String args[]) {
            myFx();
      }
}	

A	122.8
B	123
C	Compiler error.
D	Runtime error.
	<----Right Answer

Q.21: What is the output?

class Program {
      static void myFx() {
            double d=122.8;
            String str = (String) d;
            System.out.println(str);
      }
      public static void main(String args[]) {

```
            myFx();
        }
}
```

A	122.8
B	123
C	Compiler error.
D	Runtime error.
	<----Right Answer

Q.22: What is the output?

```
class Program {
        static void myFx() {
                double d=122.8;
                Object obj = (Object) d;
                System.out.println(obj);
        }
        public static void main(String args[]) {
                myFx();
        }
}
```

A	123
B	122.8
C	Compiler error.
D	Runtime error.
	<----Right Answer

Q.23: What is the output?

```
class Program {
        static void myFx() {
                boolean b=false;
                Object obj = (Object) b;
                System.out.println(obj);
        }
        public static void main(String args[]) {
                myFx();
        }
}
```

A	false.
B	Compiler error.
C	Runtime error.
D	true.
	<----Right Answer

Q.24: What is the output?

```
class Program {
        static void myFx() {
                long l=999;
                Object obj = (Object) l;
                System.out.println(obj);
        }
        public static void main(String args[]) {
                myFx();
        }
}
```

A	999
B	1000
C	Compiler error.
D	Runtime error.
	<----Right Answer

Q.25: What is the output?

```
class Program {
        static void myFx() {
                int i=199;
                Object obj = (Object) i;
                System.out.println(obj);
        }
        public static void main(String args[]) {
                myFx();
        }
}
```

A	199
B	200
C	Compiler error.
D	Runtime error.
	<----Right Answer

Answers:

Q.No	Ans	Explanation
1	C	Type conversion occurs between compatible types e.g byte to int.

2	B	Type casting occurs between different types e.g double to long.
3	C	By computation the result is 10.
4	B	By computation the result is 10.0 .
5	A	By computation the result is 10.0
6	C	It is an invalid expression.
7	B	By computation the result is 10.0 .
8	C	It is an invalid expression.
9	B	It is an invalid expression.
10	C	It is an invalid expression.
11	C	It is an invalid expression.
12	D	By computation the result is 234.0
13	D	It is an invalid expression.
14	A	By computation the result is 24.0
15	C	It is an invalid expression.
16	A	It is an invalid expression.
17	A	By computation the result is 99.
18	C	By computation the result is -126.
19	A	By computation the result is 122.
20	A	By computation the result is 122.8 .
21	C	It is an invalid expression.
22	B	By computation the result is 122.8 .
23	A	By computation the result is false.
24	A	By computation the result is 999.
25	A	By computation the result is 199.

www.ingramcontent.com/pod-product-compliance
Lightning Source LLC
La Vergne TN
LVHW060122070326
832902LV00019B/3094